The Christian Looks at Himself

Anthony A. Hoekema

THE
CHRISTIAN
LOOKS
AT
HIMSELF

by

ANTHONY A. HOEKEMA, 1913-

William B. Eerdmans Publishing Company

Copyright © 1975 William B. Eerdmans Pub. Co.
Grand Rapids, Mich.

All Rights Reserved

Printed in the United States of America

First edition, 1975
Second edition, 1977

Library of Congress Cataloging in Publication Data

Hoekema, Anthony A   1913-
    The Christian looks at himself.

    Bibliography: p. 143.
    Includes index.
    1. Man (Theology) 2. Christian life—Reformed authors. 3.
Christianity—Psychology. I. Title.
BT701.2.H62   248'.4   75-1285
ISBN 0-8028-1595-2

Unless otherwise noted, Scripture quotations are from the Revised
Standard Version, and are used by permission.

Quotations from *Life Together* by Dietrich Bonhoeffer are re-
printed by permission of Harper & Row. Copyright, 1954, by
Harper & Row, Publishers, Inc.

45,67a

To the
CHRISTIAN ASSOCIATION FOR
PSYCHOLOGICAL STUDIES

Contents

7

Preface

The main purpose of this book is to examine what Scripture says about the way Christians ought to see themselves and their fellow Christians, and to suggest various ways in which these insights can be implemented.

The self-image seems to be a popular topic these days. Books like *I'm OK—You're OK* by Thomas A. Harris stress the value of a positive self-image, but do so on a purely humanistic basis. I'm concerned to deal with this problem in a distinctively Christian way, and to show that the Bible teaches us to have a positive image of ourselves because we are new creatures in Christ. The Christian self-image, therefore, involves looking at ourselves and at our fellow Christians with the eyes of faith.

The plan of the book is as follows: The introduction states the nature of the problem and indicates why a specifically Christian treatment of this topic is needed. Part I, which follows, deals with the biblical background for the positive self-image of the Christian. Various Scripture passages are examined to see what they teach us about the way a Christian should view himself and his fellow believers. In Part II suggestions are made for the implementation of these biblical teachings by preachers, counselors, teachers, and parents. What all this means for the development and deepening of genuine Christian fellowship is explored in a closing chapter.

Unless otherwise noted, all Scripture quotations are from the Revised Standard Version. Facts of publication for books and articles mentioned in the text will be found in the bibliography.

The topic of the Christian self-image has a particular fascination for me because of my interest in both psychology and theology. The immediate occasion for writing this book, however, was an invitation to give a paper on the Christian self-image for the 1971 convention of the Christian Association for Psychological Studies, held in Milwaukee, Wisconsin. I wish therefore to acknowledge my indebtedness to that association and to its executive secretary, William L. Hiemstra, for getting me started on this subject.

I should like to express my gratitude to the Board of Trustees of Calvin Theological Seminary for granting me a year's sabbatical leave, during which this book was written, and to the staff of the Cambridge University Library for the use of their facilities.

I should also like to acknowledge the help received from many writers in the area of my topic, and from students, colleagues, and friends with whom the subject was discussed. Above all, I owe thanks to my wife, Ruth, for her invaluable support and help during the writing of this book.

May the Lord use this study to help many people see more fully what it means to be a new creature in Christ.

Cambridge, England　　　　　　　ANTHONY A. HOEKEMA
January, 1974

THE
CHRISTIAN
LOOKS
AT
HIMSELF

Introduction: The Problem and the Need

How should a Christian think about himself? Should his self-image be primarily negative or positive? Should a Christian, in thinking about himself, lay primary stress on his continued sinfulness? Or should his primary emphasis be on his newness in Christ?

This is the problem with which I plan to deal in this book: the problem of the Christian self-image. By "self-image" I mean something virtually synonymous with what is designated by the psychological term "self-esteem." Stanley Coopersmith, in his valuable study entitled *Antecedents of Self-esteem*, defines that term as follows: "By self-esteem we refer to the evaluation which the individual makes and customarily maintains with regard to himself: it expresses an attitude of approval or disapproval, and indicates the extent to which the individual believes himself to be capable, significant, successful, and worthy" (pp. 4-5). It will be seen that, according to this definition, one's self-esteem may be either high or low. In this book the term "self-image" will be used to designate the way in which a person regards himself, his conception of his own worth.

13

One's self-image, therefore, may also be either high or low, either predominantly positive or predominantly negative.

It will be generally granted, I believe, that what someone thinks of himself has much to do with the kind of life he will live. A person who sees himself as inferior to others will probably do inferior work, whereas a person who believes himself to be more capable than others will probably do better work. A man tends to live up to his self-image.

Recent psychological studies have confirmed this observation. Both Coopersmith (in *Antecedents*) and Abraham Maslow (in his *Toward a Psychology of Being*) conclude on the basis of research that people with low self-esteem tend to be less creative and more anxious, and are less likely to have successful experiences, than persons with high self-esteem. Conversely, people with high self-esteem were found to be generally more creative, more poised, more effective, and less anxious than those with low self-esteem.

That a child's self-image has much to do with the level of his or her performance is something every teacher has observed. There was, for example, the imaginative Iowa teacher who decided to dramatize the black-white problem by dividing her third-grade pupils into blue-eyed and brown-eyed children. One Friday the brown-eyed children were seated in the back of the room, while the teacher kept saying to the blue-eyed children in front: "Brown-eyed children can't read as well as you can, can't color as well as you can, are not as bright as you are"—and the like. That day the brown-eyed children did not do as well in school as the blue-eyed children. They believed their teacher and lived up to their poor self-image.

The following Monday the roles were reversed. The

blue-eyed children now sat at the back of the room. The teacher said repeatedly, "Blue-eyed children can't read as well as brown-eyed children, can't do sums as well as brown-eyed children, are not as bright as brown-eyed children" —and so on. That day, as can be imagined, the blue-eyed children did not do as well as the brown-eyed children, nor as well as they had done on the preceding Friday. Something happened to their performance because something had happened to their self-image.

Obviously, a predominantly negative self-image has evil consequences for adults as well as for children. One of the major social problems of our time is the treatment of minority groups in a community or nation. Black writers like James Baldwin have reminded us that one of the most crucial aspects of the problem of racism in America is the question of the black man's self-image. Many black people in America have in the past come to think of themselves as actually inferior to others, since this was the way they were looked upon by white people, and since they had been led to accept the white man's image of the black man as correct. As a result, there developed among black people a psychology of inferiority, accompanied by anxiety and fear as well as anger and rage. Black people are now rebelling against this belittlement, refusing any longer to accept the white man's negative image of themselves as true. There was the black boy who put up a banner in his room which read, "I'M ME AND I'M GOOD, 'CAUSE GOD DON'T MAKE JUNK."

All this having been said, it would seem that people who accept the Christian view of man as a creature made in God's image and redeemed from sin by the sacrifice of God's own Son would have, for the most part, a very positive self-image. Unfortunately, however, this is by no means the case. Conservative evangelical Christians often have a rather negative self-image.

A number of factors may account for this. From many an evangelical pulpit hearers are continually reminded of their depravity and worthlessness. In an article entitled "The Nature of Man and the Christian's Self-esteem" (*Journal of Psychology and Theology,* January, 1973), William M. Counts remarks that he was once told by a clergyman, "I feel I've preached an effective sermon when I've left my congregation feeling guilty" (p. 38). If the message of guilt and sinfulness is not balanced by the biblical message of forgiveness and renewal, such preaching may indeed create in the hearers a negative self-image which may take years to erase.

Some of the hymns of the church have made their contribution to the negative self-image often found among Christians. In my younger days we used to sing a version of the hymn "Beneath the Cross of Jesus" which went like this, in the second stanza:

> *And from my smitten heart with tears,*
> *Two wonders I confess:*
> *The wonders of His glorious love*
> *And my own worthlessness.*

Fortunately, in the hymnal presently used in our church, the last line has been changed to read, "And my unworthiness." I quite agree that we are unworthy; I do not believe it accords with biblical teaching to say that we are worthless.

Though we can understand the contrast intended in the

following lines between the unfathomable love of Christ and our own unworthiness, still Isaac Watts' famous hymn could convey to many people a quite unflattering self-image:

> *Alas, and did my Saviour bleed?*
> *And did my Sovereign die?*
> *Would he devote that sacred head*
> *For such a worm as I?*

In some of the official formularies used by evangelical Christian churches one finds sentences in which believers are urged to "loathe" or to "abhor" themselves. Again the terminology is unfortunate. Whereas all Christians would agree that we must abhor our sins and loathe our continuing sinfulness, I do not believe that the Scriptures require us to abhor and loathe *ourselves*.

Others have noted the tendency among Christians toward a negative self-image. It is probably Roman Catholic Christians in particular whom Jean-Paul Sartre is caricaturing when in his play *The Flies* he makes a man fall on his knees saying, "I stink! Oh, how I stink! I am a mass of rottenness.... I have sinned a thousand times, I am a sink of ordure, and I reek to heaven!" After this pretty little speech Zeus, the character who stands for God in the play, comments, "O worthy man!" Here Sartre, the atheist, is telling us: this is how I see Christians, as always groveling in the dust because of their sins—and the more they do this, the more their God is pleased. Even after we have made the necessary allowances for exaggeration, there is probably enough truth in Sartre's picture of the self-abnegating Christian to make us all wince a little.

If we who claim to be Christians are honest with ourselves, we shall have to admit that many of us tend to have a self-image that over-accentuates the negative. Many of us commonly see ourselves through the purple-colored glasses of our depravity—sometimes even called "total depravity." I do not deny that according to the Scriptures we are all by nature depraved or sinful in every aspect of our being, but the same Scriptures teach us about redemption and renewal. Sad to say, however, many of us tend to look only at our depravity and not at our renewal. We have been writing our continuing sinfulness in capital letters, and our newness in Christ in small letters. We believe in our depravity so strongly we think we have to practice it, while we hardly dare to believe in our newness.

William Counts cites the example of a young woman he once counseled whose experience, he adds, is unfortunately much too common:

> As a college student, she embraced a conservative "fundamentalist" type of Christianity, with a heavy emphasis on human sinfulness. She came to see she was a "sinner," and that her hope for salvation was "the blood of Christ." She became a leader among her Christian friends, and planned to become a foreign missionary. Before she embarked on her missionary career, she did some graduate study in psychology and had a brief career in social work.

> Here, as she encountered the writings of Maslow, Rogers, and others, she began to suspect her Christian teaching. She discarded some of her previous ideas. She started viewing herself as a worthy person. She threw off the notions of sin and depravity. Soon she was a freer, happier, more healthy person than she had been before she embraced Christianity. She began to feel "released." Her tension and guilt began to vanish. Her family welcomed the return of her old

happy self. Yet she regained her former happiness only at
the cost of discarding her basic Christian beliefs. (p. 38)

Unfortunately, incidents of this sort create a dilemma
for Christian psychotherapists—and, we might add, for
Christian theologians, pastors, and teachers. It would
seem that people like this young woman have only two
choices: either retain the Christian faith and have a neu-
rotic personality with a predominantly negative self-image,
or have a healthy personality and a positive self-image at
the cost of rejecting the Christian faith. On the basis of
this young woman's experience it would appear impossible
to embrace the Christian faith and to have a positive self-
image at the same time.

Humanistic psychologists have, in fact, devised their own
solution to this problem—a solution which is comparable
to that adopted by the young woman just described. Men
like Erich Fromm, Abraham Maslow, and Carl Rogers
maintain that human nature is basically neutral or good,
capable of making the right choices at any time. This view
of human nature, it is then affirmed, provides the kind of
foundation for positive self-esteem and for a positive self-
image which traditional Christian teaching about man does
not and cannot provide. Note, for example, how Maslow
describes what he calls the "inner nature" of man:

> We have, each of us, an essential biologically based inner
> nature, which is to some degree "natural," intrinsic, given,
> and, in a certain limited sense, unchangeable, or, at least,
> unchanging.
> . . . This inner nature, as much as we know of it so far,
> seems not to be intrinsically or primarily or necessarily evil.
> The basic needs . . . the basic human emotions and the
> basic human capacities are on their face either neutral, pre-

moral or positively good.... Human nature is not nearly as bad as it has been thought to be. In fact it can be said that the possibilities of human nature have customarily been sold short.

Since this inner nature is good or neutral rather than bad, it is best to bring it out and to encourage it rather than to suppress it. If it is permitted to guide our life, we grow healthy, fruitful, and happy. (*Toward a Psychology of Being,* second edition, pp. 3-4)

The view of man held by these psychologists does seem to hold promise of providing the basis for a positive self-image. Yet we may raise some serious questions about the philosophical background which lies behind this view. Psychologists like Fromm, Maslow, and Rogers hold basically to an evolutionistic understanding of the origin of man. Their theory of man is not specifically based on biblical teachings. One might well question, therefore, whether they would accept the biblical view that man is the product of a special creative act of God, made in the image of his Creator. One might well wonder whether these writers believe that man is destined to continue to exist after death in an immortal state. One might well have his doubts about whether the uniqueness of man in the universe can be sufficiently maintained in such philosophical systems as are the foundation for contemporary humanism.

It cannot be denied, of course, that one can ascribe considerable significance to man under a humanist philosophy. Under such a system of thought man can still be urged to strive for a better world, to do the hard right instead of the easy wrong, to love his fellowman. A humanist could well consider man to be the culmination of a long evolutionary process which has led over the centuries to ever higher levels of existence. One certainly could build a positive self-image on a view of man as the apex of long ages of evolutionary progress.

Though we may grant, however, that psychologies rooted in a humanistic view of man do give some basis for a positive self-image, we must go on to observe that the Christian faith, far from inevitably implying a negative self-image, has resources for building a positive self-image which far transcend those which a humanist philosophy can provide.

To begin with, the Scriptures, which are basic to the Christian faith, teach that man came into existence through a special creative act of God and that in distinction from all other creatures he alone has been made in the image of God. This means that man stands in a unique relationship to God, to his fellowmen, and to the cosmos. Of all God's creatures, man alone has the capacity to worship his Creator, to serve Him, to enter into covenant partnership with Him, and to love Him. But man was also created with the capacity for loving and serving his fellowmen, enabling him to live for others instead of for self, and in this way to find his own life enriched and fulfilled. In addition, God has given man dominion over the earth, implying that man is to rule over the entire cosmos as God's representative. This implies not just the cultivation of the earth's soil and the mining of its resources, but also the development of science and art, and even the exploration of space. It will be evident, therefore, that in the Christian view man is a being of unique significance, the capstone of God's creation.

The Bible also teaches, however, that man fell from his original state of uprightness when he disobeyed God's commandment (Gen. 3). Does this mean that man now became a being of no worth? Nothing could be further from the truth. Even after the fall man was still considered to be a creature of infinite worth. Jesus said that one human life is worth more than the whole world (Matt. 16:26). The Scriptures also affirm that even fallen man still bears the image of God (Gen. 9:6, James 3:9).

The continuing worth of man after the fall is particularly evident in the Bible's teaching on redemption. God did not leave man in his sin, but He "gave his only Son, that whoever believes in him should not perish but have eternal life" (John 3:16). Surely God would not give His Son for creatures He considered to be of little worth! Peter, in fact, put it this way: "You know that you were ransomed from the futile ways inherited from your fathers, not with perishable things such as silver or gold, but with the precious blood of Christ, like that of a lamb without blemish or spot" (I Pet. 1:18-19). Not only did God redeem His people at so infinite a price; He continues to preserve them in so meticulous a way that the very hairs of their heads are numbered (Luke 12:7).

To this should be added a consideration of the results of the redemptive process in the lives of believers. When God by His Holy Spirit regenerates a person, that person becomes a new creature in Christ. This means that the believer, no longer enslaved by sin, is now a joyful servant of Christ. Old things have passed away; all things have become new. Though this does not mean that the believer is now completely rid of sin and lives a life of sinless perfection, it does mean, as will be shown more fully later, that what is most distinctive about him is not the old life of sin but the new life he has in Christ. Accordingly, the believer must see himself primarily in terms of this new life, and not in terms of his continuing depravity and failure. "So you also must consider yourselves dead to sin and alive to God in Christ Jesus" (Rom. 6:11).

We see, then, that the Christian faith does indeed have tremendous resources for building a positive self-image. When it happens, as in the case of the young woman mentioned above, that a Christian grows up with a primarily negative self-image, this may well be due to causes which were prior in origin to any doctrinal teaching or theological awareness. Yet such a negative self-image may also come from a distorted understanding of biblical doctrines, in which primary emphasis is laid on the guilt and sinfulness of man rather than on the redemptive work of God for man and in man. When, on the other hand, the Christian faith is properly understood and is embraced in its totality, the Christian believer should have a basically positive self-image. When Christian teaching is properly apprehended, the dilemma described above does not really exist. It is not a question of *either* the Christian faith *or* a positive self-image. Rather, when the Christian faith is accepted in its totality, that faith brings with it a predominantly positive self-image. To demonstrate that this is so will be the main purpose of this book.

PART I: THE BIBLICAL BACKGROUND

CHAPTER ONE
Paul's Self-Image

Before taking a look at specific New Testament passages which deal directly with the way a believer should look at himself, let us try to get at our subject in a somewhat indirect way. When we read through Paul's epistles we cannot fail to sense that, though deeply conscious of his sinfulness and keenly aware of his continuing imperfection, Paul nevertheless had a predominantly positive self-image. It will therefore be helpful for us first of all to take a careful look at the way Paul viewed himself, as a concrete illustration of what a healthy Christian self-image can be and ought to be.

Paul often saw himself as a great sinner. But he never described himself as a sinner without at the same time referring to the grace of God which forgave his sins, accepted him, and enabled him to be useful in God's kingdom. In other words, Paul never simply sat down to brood about his offenses; whenever he thought about his sin, he thought about the grace of God! In I Timothy 1:15, for example, he calls himself the chief or foremost of sinners, but he does this in a context in which he is describing the salva-

25

tion Christ has come into the world to bring—a salvation of which Paul knows himself to be a grateful partaker: "Faithful is the saying, and worthy of all acceptation, that Christ Jesus came into the world to save sinners, of whom I am chief" (ASV). The point of Ephesians 3:8 is the contrast between Paul's feeling of unworthiness and the privileged position to which God has called him: "To me, though I am the very least of all the saints, this grace was given, to preach to the Gentiles the unsearchable riches of Christ." In I Corinthians 15:9-10 Paul gives expression to his deep regret at his having once been a persecutor of the church; yet he maintains a positive self-image because of what the grace of God has done for him: "For I am the least of the apostles, unfit to be called an apostle, because I persecuted the church of God. But by the grace of God I am what I am, and his grace toward me was not in vain. On the contrary, I worked harder than any of them, though it was not I, but the grace of God which is with me."

Though Paul can look back to episodes in his former life of which he is now ashamed, he does not continue to brood on these matters; he has learned to "forget what lies behind" (Phil. 3:13). Without for a moment glossing over the seriousness of his past sins, Paul sees that where sin increased, grace abounded all the more: "I thank him who has given me strength for this, Christ Jesus our Lord, because he judged me faithful by appointing me to his service, though I formerly blasphemed and persecuted and insulted him; but I received mercy because I had acted ignorantly in unbelief, and the grace of our Lord overflowed for me with the faith and love that are in Christ Jesus" (I Tim. 1:12-14).

We may say, then, that though Paul does have a very deep sense of sin, he also is able to maintain a predominantly positive self-image. Yet his confidence is not so much in himself as in God, who enables him to do whatever he does. Because Paul often makes positive statements about himself, he is sometimes accused of pride. I cannot agree with this judgment; a careful study of his epistles will reveal that whenever Paul speaks about his achievements, he always gives God the praise. ". . . It was not I, but the grace of God which is with me" (I Cor. 15:10). "Such is the confidence that we have through Christ toward God. Not that we are sufficient of ourselves to claim anything as coming from us; our sufficiency is from God" (II Cor. 3:4-5). "But we have this treasure in earthen vessels, to show that the transcendent power belongs to God and not to us" (II Cor. 4:7).

As a matter of fact, in II Corinthians 11:30 Paul goes so far as to say, "If I must boast, I will boast of the things that show my weakness." He follows this puzzling statement with an intriguing reference to an incident from his past life: "At Damascus, the governor under King Aretas guarded the city of Damascus in order to seize me, but I was let down in a basket through a window in the wall and escaped his hands" (vv. 32-33). One may well wonder why Paul would bother to mention this incident at all. Most people would say nothing to anybody about so inglorious an exit from a city. To understand why Paul mentions this episode, we must remember that his enemies in Corinth were trying to discredit his apostleship. Look at this man Paul, these enemies were saying; is he not a pitiable figure? "His letters are weighty and strong, but his bodily presence is weak . . ." (10:10). In reply to this criticism, the apostle is here telling the Corinthians: In one respect my enemies are right. I agree with them that I am not a very imposing person. If you were to think of me as such a person, you would be praising me instead of God, and I don't want you to do that. I would rather have you think of me as an ordinary kind of person strengthened by Christ. In fact, I don't really mind having you think of me, at least occasionally, as a kind of comic figure—which I certainly was when I escaped from Damascus by riding in a basket. The point is this: The secret of my apostleship and the dynamic of my life is not to be found in my own strong personal qualities but rather in the fact that I am and continue to be a man empowered by Christ.

Paul now goes on, in chapter 12, to recount the story of his "thorn in the flesh." Though we are not told exactly what this thorn was, it seems most likely that it was some kind of physical affliction. Three times, says Paul, I prayed that this thorn might be removed, but each time the answer was no. What the Lord then said to me was this: "My grace is sufficient for you, for my power is made perfect in weakness" (12:9). The Lord did not take away this thorn because He wished to keep me from relying on my own strength (which I might otherwise be sorely tempted to do) and because He wanted me to lean solely on Him for strength. Paul therefore concludes by saying, "I will all the more gladly boast of my weaknesses, that the power of Christ may rest upon me. For the sake of Christ, then, I am content with weaknesses, insults, hardships, persecutions, and calamities; for when I am weak, then I am strong" (12:9-10).

Yet, while giving God all the glory for what he was and

for what he had done, Paul did not just brush aside his considerable achievements with a wave of the hand. He dared to say, "I worked harder than any of them [the other apostles]" (I Cor. 15:10). To the Ephesian elders he said, "I did not shrink from declaring to you the whole counsel of God" (Acts 20:27). And as his life was nearing its end, he wrote to Timothy, "I have fought the good fight, I have finished the race, I have kept the faith" (II Tim. 4:7).

Paul realized that he had not yet attained perfection: "Not that I have already obtained this or am already perfect. . . . I press on toward the goal for the prize of the upward call of God in Christ Jesus" (Phil. 3:12, 14). In spite of this fact, however—and I find this one of the most fascinating facets of Paul's personality—he dared to say on more than one occasion to the believers who would receive his letters, "I urge you, then, be imitators of me" (I Cor. 4:16, 11:1, Phil. 3:17, II Thess. 3:7). Most of us, I am sure, would prefer to say to our children, our friends, or our associates, "Do as I say, but not as I do." Not many of us would dare to hold up our own lives as examples to others, as models which others should imitate. These passages, we must admit, certainly do reveal a positive self-image. Conscious of the fact that he was not perfect, and that whatever good there was in him was due to God's grace, Paul was yet so confident that the Holy Spirit would continue to empower him to do God's will that he had the courage to say to others, "Be imitators of me."

Though one can find in Paul's writings many descriptions of the depths of man's sinfulness, yet he did not write about man's depravity in order to demean man. His purpose was always to celebrate the liberating power of the gospel. And so, while recognizing himself to be a sinner, he at the same time rejoiced in his total forgiveness. While realizing that there were impulses and tendencies in him which he continually had to fight, he knew that in Christ he could win the victory. While he was willing to say, not just "I was" but "I am" the chief of sinners, Paul nevertheless saw himself as a new creature in Christ.

Summing up, we may say that Paul, despite his deep sense of sin, had a positive self-image. He saw himself as a person upon whom God had showered His grace, whom God had enabled and was still enabling to live a fruitful life for Christ, and whom God so continued to fill with His Spirit that his life could be an example to others.

CHAPTER TWO

The Exhilaration of Forgiveness

When we turn specifically to the Scriptures to see what they teach us about the way a believer should look at himself, we must first of all note what the Bible says about the question of sin and guilt. For surely nothing contributes so much to a negative self-image as a deep feeling of guilt.

That this is so is amply demonstrated in literature. We noted in the previous chapter the character in Sartre's *The Flies* who grovels in the dust because of his excessive guilt-feelings. Raskolnikov, in Dostoievsky's *Crime and Punishment,* commits a crime in order to improve his self-image, but in the end he finds his self-esteem restored only when he goes to Siberia to suffer for his crime and in this way "atone" for his guilt. The classic literary illustration of the devastating effects of unresolved guilt-feelings is, I suppose, Lady Macbeth in Shakespeare's *Macbeth:* "Oh, all the perfumes of Arabia will not sweeten this little hand!"

But obviously we need not restrict ourselves to literary illustrations. All of us have had enough experience with unresolved guilt-feelings to know what they do to our self-image. When one is obsessed with guilt-feelings, he despises himself, feels utterly worthless, and is likely to plunge into a nightmare of despair.

Though some contemporary theologians affirm that modern man is no longer troubled by feelings of guilt, psychiatrists and clinical psychologists know better. For the problem of unresolved guilt-feelings is one of the most common problems with which they must deal. It will be granted, of course, that guilt-feelings are not as common in our contemporary permissive society as they were in earlier days, when the existence of objective moral standards was more generally recognized than it is now. Today "estrangement" would seem to be a more common feeling than "guilt." Yet it remains true that enough people are troubled by guilt-feelings in today's world so that this continues to be a significant problem. And it must not be forgotten that many persons who say that they have no guilt-feelings may nevertheless reveal the presence of such feelings in various unrecognized ways.

What, then, do the Scriptures teach about the problem of guilt and guilt-feelings? The first thing we should note is that the Bible deepens the problem, making our guilt a much more serious matter than we might have thought it was. For it shows us that when we do wrong we sin not just against other people but against God Himself. David's words in Psalm 51 here spring to mind. Though his double sin of adultery and murder had certainly been committed against other human beings, nevertheless David cries out, "Against thee, thee only, have I sinned, and done that which is evil in thy sight" (v. 4). The so-called "second table of the law" teaches us that such sins as murder, adultery, lying, and theft are sins against God as well as man. Our guilt is therefore much worse than we thought: it is not just that we have hurt men; we have offended God!

The Bible further teaches that no man is free from guilt. "There is none that does good, no, not one," says the author of Psalm 14. After quoting these words in Romans 3, Paul sums it all up by saying, " . . . All have sinned, and fall short of the glory of God" (v. 23). In the light of the Scriptures every one of us is guilty of having sinned against God and of having done things that are highly displeasing to Him.

But after having deepened the problem of guilt, the Bible goes on to show how God has provided a way whereby we can be delivered not only from *feelings* of guilt but from guilt itself. "For God so loved the world that he gave his only Son, that whoever believes in him should not perish but have eternal life. For God sent the Son into the world, not to condemn the world, but that the world might be saved through him" (John 3:16-17).

What is important to note here is the principle of substitution. God removes our guilt not just by overlooking it, as an indulgent parent might overlook the naughtiness of his child, but by providing a substitute who suffers and dies for our transgressions. Paul describes all this in the third chapter of Romans. After having said what he did about the universality of sin, he goes on to say, "They [believers] are justified by his grace as a gift, through the redemption which is in Christ Jesus, whom God put forward as an expiation by his blood, to be received by faith" (vv. 24-25). The word here translated "justified" means to be acquitted by God, to be considered as perfectly righteous, to be completely freed from guilt. The word rendered "expiation" describes a transaction in which the guilt of one person is atoned for by another. The Greek translation of the Old Testament used this word to designate the lid on the ark of the covenant, which was sprinkled with the blood of the sin-offering on the Day of Atonement to show that the sins of the people could be removed only through the shedding of blood. When Paul now applies this word to Christ, he indicates that our guilt has been removed by the shedding of Christ's blood on the cross. God can therefore now with perfect justice take away the guilt of His people (v. 26), since Christ as our substitute has shed His blood for us and thus borne the penalties of our sin for us. This does not mean, as is often popularly supposed, that God the Father hated us, but Christ loved us and by His atoning death changed the Father's hatred into love. For Paul makes clear in verse 25 that it was the Father Himself who, when He sent His Son into the world, provided the expiatory sacrifice which is the judicial basis for the removal of our guilt. Thus the cross of Christ is a revelation both of God's righteousness and of His love.

The principle of substitution is taught also in II Corinthians 5:21: "For our sake he made him to be sin who knew no sin, so that in him we might become the righteousness of God." Christ identified himself with our sin, Paul here teaches, so that we might now be able to identify ourselves with the righteousness of God—that is, so that we might now stand before God as perfectly righteous because we are one with Christ. Crystal clear on this matter is verse 19 of this same chapter: "God was in Christ reconciling the world to himself, not counting their trespasses against them."

The upshot of this is that a person who believes in Jesus Christ and is therefore truly one with Him should no longer be troubled by feelings of guilt. Such a person, having confessed his sins to God and having asked for forgiveness on the basis of the work of Christ, is assured by Scripture that his guilt has been taken away. Since all his guilt has been borne by Christ as his substitute, the believer does not have to bear it any longer. Guilt, therefore, should no longer be a problem in his life. When he does something wrong, he should of course at once confess his sin to God and to the person whom he has wronged, making restitution if necessary. But feelings of guilt toward God he should be done with forever.

So it ought to be. Unfortunately, however, many Christian believers still have a great deal of trouble with guilt-feelings. Speaking on the subject of "Christian Freedom" in a lecture in Cambridge, England, Canon Michael Green of St. John's College, Nottingham, said, "Many Christians do not rejoice because of their freedom from guilt." Christians, he went on to say, ought to be the happiest of men since their guilt has been completely taken away by Christ; yet many of them are a dismal lot, registering gloom instead of joy. They should be rid of guilt-feelings, but often they are ridden by them.

Why should this be? Why should people who have accepted the Christian faith still be troubled by guilt-feelings? One answer is that such people have failed either to grasp fully or to accept fully the glad tidings of the gospel. They don't take God at His Word. They have distorted the Christian message. They have changed the

liberating gospel of grace into a system of legalistic bondage in which freedom from guilt depends on the number
of good works one has done. Refusing to lean wholly on
Christ for salvation, such people are really leaning on themselves, and failing to find peace of mind.

People of this sort will probably not be able to get rid
of their guilt-feelings without counseling or psychotherapy.
It is not my purpose in this book to prescribe in detail
the kinds of counseling techniques which might be helpful to such people. I am, however, concerned to point out
what the Bible teaches about the removal of guilt.

We begin with some Old Testament passages. David in
Psalm 32 celebrates the joy of the forgiveness of sins when
he writes:

> *Blessed is he whose transgression is forgiven,*
> *whose sin is covered.*
> *Blessed is the man to whom the Lord imputes*
> *no iniquity. . . .* (vv. 1-2)

In Psalm 103 David praises God for the exhilaration of
total forgiveness:

> *Bless the Lord, O my soul,*
> *and forget not all his benefits,*
> *who forgives all your iniquity,*
> *who heals all your diseases. . . .*
> *He does not deal with us according to our sins,*
> *nor requite us according to our iniquities. . . .*
> *As far as the east is from the west,*
> *so far does he remove our transgressions from us.*
> (vv. 2, 3, 10, 12)

Other Old Testament writers speak of the blessing of the
forgiveness of sins. Isaiah, for example, writes as follows:

I, I am He
   who blots out your transgressions for my own
   sake,
and I will not remember your sins. (43:25)

In the next chapter he compares God's removal of our sins with the way the morning sun does away with the mists of the night:

I have swept away your transgressions like a cloud,
   and your sins like mist. (44:22)

Unforgettably beautiful are the words of Micah in the seventh chapter of his prophecy:

>*Who is a God like thee, pardoning iniquity*
>   *and passing over transgression*
>   *for the remnant of his inheritance?*
>*He does not retain his anger for ever*
>   *because he delights in steadfast love.*
>*He will again have compassion upon us,*
>   *he will tread our iniquities under foot.*
>*Thou wilt cast all our sins*
>   *into the depths of the sea.* (7:18-19)

When we turn to the New Testament, we find Christ Himself teaching in the clearest of words that a person who believes in Him will never be condemned on account of his sins: "For God so loved the world that he gave his only Son, that whoever believes in him should not perish but have eternal life" (John 3:16). "Truly, truly, I say to you, he who hears my words and believes him who sent me, has eternal life; he does not come into judgment, but has passed from death to life" (John 5:24).

In the Book of Acts we find many apostolic addresses setting forth the way of salvation for both Jewish and Gentile hearers. To single out just one of these, note how Paul in his sermon to the Jews at Antioch of Pisidia affirms that the deliverance from guilt which they were fruitlessly trying to obtain by obeying the Mosaic law could be received through faith in Jesus Christ: "Let it be known to you therefore, brethren, that through this man [Jesus] forgiveness of sins is proclaimed to you, and by him every one that believes is freed from everything from which you could not be freed by the law of Moses" (Acts 13:38-39).

Turning now to Paul's epistles, we find an abundance of passages celebrating the believer's joy at his acquittal from guilt. We can look at only a few. The triumphant affirmation of Romans 5:1 is well known: "Therefore, since we are justified by faith, we have peace with God through our Lord Jesus Christ." Paul begins his magnificent eighth chapter of Romans with these comforting words: "There is therefore now no condemnation for those who are in Christ Jesus." Note too how decisively Paul dismisses the fear that someone might possibly still bring charges of guilt against God's people: "Who shall bring any charge against God's elect? It is God who justifies; who is to condemn?" (Rom. 8:33-34). See how joyfully he proclaims the certainty of our forgiveness in Ephesians 1:7-8: "In him [Jesus Christ] we have redemption through his blood, the forgiveness of our trespasses, according to the riches of his grace which he lavished upon us."

It would not be difficult to find many more New Testament passages setting forth the happy message of forgiveness. The main purpose of the Book of Hebrews is to set forth Christ as the great High Priest who has once and for all taken away our sins: " . . . He has appeared once for all at the end of the age to put away sin by the sacrifice of himself" (9:26). Often quoted as a passage conveying assurance of pardon to all who repent are the words of I John 1:9: "If we confess our sins, he is faithful and just, and will forgive our sins and cleanse us from all unrighteousness." The very last book of the Bible, in fact, contains a doxology to the one who has forever set us free from guilt: "To him who loves us and has freed us from our sins by his blood and made us a kingdom, priests to his God and Father, to him be glory and dominion for ever and ever. Amen" (Rev. 1:5-6).

What a liberating truth this is! When one is in Christ, these passages tell us, there is no condemnation for him, his sins have all been forgiven, and all his guilt has been removed. God now looks upon him as no longer guilty but as clothed with the perfect righteousness of Jesus Christ. His sins have been cast into the depths of the sea, and he can now joyfully sing,

> *My sin—O the bliss of this glorious thought—*
> *My sin, not in part but the whole,*
> *Is nailed to the cross, and I bear it no more.*
> *Praise the Lord, praise the Lord, O my soul!*

What has been developed in this chapter is basic to forming a positive self-image. One cannot have a positive self-image while believing himself to be laden with guilt and hence liable to condemnation. We see, therefore, the importance of the biblical teaching on the removal of guilt. It is, as we have seen, always possible for people so to distort the biblical message as to lay the emphasis on sin and guilt and to play down or deny altogether the good news of forgiveness. But when one grasps the message of the Scriptures in its totality, he will know that although the Bible does teach us about sin, its main emphasis is on the grace of God which takes away our sin.

The confident acceptance of our forgiveness, the exhilaration of knowing that God accepts us and loves us in spite of our shortcomings and failures, is the foundation for a positive self-image.

CHAPTER THREE
Old and New Man

But, someone may still say, what about our "sinful nature"? What about our "depravity"? Does not the Bible teach that even after we have been born again, even after we have become believers, we continue to have a sinful nature and therefore to keep on sinning? And does this not imply that the Bible teaches us to continue to have a negative image of ourselves even after we have been converted?

In fact, such a person might go on to say, even when I accept the fact that in Christ all my past sins have been forgiven and all my past guilt has been removed, if I am as bad a sinner as the Bible describes me to be, don't I keep on increasing my sins and piling up my guilt every day? Though, to be sure, I confess these new sins daily and receive forgiveness for them, doesn't all this add up to a pretty negative self-image? Mustn't I continue to see myself as a person perpetually dogged by failure, constantly trying to do the right things but just as constantly failing to do them? If the very holiest of men, as one Christian creed puts it, have only "a small beginning of this obedience," how can any believer avoid having a negative image of himself?

This is the problem with which we must now deal. In trying to find a solution to it, let us first of all consider what the Scriptures teach about the concepts "old man" and "new man." A better understanding of these concepts than is sometimes held will, I believe, help us to answer the question posed above.

It has been rather commonly held by Christians that in the believer there is a continual struggle between two aspects of his being, the "old man" which he is by nature and the "new man" which he puts on at the time of regeneration and conversion. According to this view, the old man and the new man are distinguishable "parts" of the believer. Before conversion he is only an old man; at the time of conversion he is said to put on the new man— without, however, totally losing the old man. The converted person, or believer, is understood to be partly new man and partly old man. At times the old man is in control, whereas at other times the new man is in the saddle; the struggle of life, therefore, is the struggle between these two aspects or parts of his being (also sometimes called the "new nature" and the "old nature").

This understanding of the old and the new man can easily lead to a negative self-image. One may, of course, think of himself as primarily new man, and only secondarily old man, but even in such a case his self-image will be of a person who is partly new and partly old—partly obedient to God and partly in rebellion against God. One might, however, also think of himself much more pessimistically, as primarily old man and only occasionally and rarely new man—in which case his self-image would be negative indeed.

It is to be seriously questioned, however, whether the view of "old man" and "new man" described above is the right one. In his *Principles of Conduct,* John Murray has rejected the idea that the believer is both old man and new man. It is just as wrong to call the believer both a new man and an old man, he argues, as it is to say that he is both regenerate and unregenerate (p. 218). Murray contends that since according to New Testament teaching the believer has put off the old man and put on the new, we must think of him as a new man—though a new man not yet made perfect, and still the subject of progressive renewal. This renewal, however, is not to be conceived of as the progressive putting off of the old man and putting on of the new (pp. 218-19).

In his study *Paul,* Herman Ridderbos offers an interpretation similar to Murray's. When Paul speaks about the old man and the new man, writes Ridderbos, he is not concerned primarily with the change which takes place in the life of an individual Christian after conversion, but with what took place once and for all in Christ (pp. 63-64). Christ, as the second Adam, died on the cross and arose from the grave for His people. Since Christ's people are one with Him in corporate unity, what happened to Christ has therefore also happened to His people. By His death on the cross Christ dealt a death-blow to sin as the power which had been enslaving His people; by His resurrection He opened up a new way of living for His people: the way of living associated with God's new creation.

The "old man" and "the new man," Ridderbos claims, ought to be understood in this salvation-history setting.

They designate the great transition from spiritual death to spiritual life which came into existence through the death and resurrection of Christ, and which is now to be appropriated by faith. In other words, we may think of these concepts in both an objective and a subjective way. Objectively, "old" and "new" man mean that in Christ's death and resurrection the old, sinful way of living has once for all been done away with, having lost its power over Christ's people, whereas the new way of living associated with God's new creation has once for all been inaugurated. Subjectively, "old" and "new" man mean that believers enter into this new way of living as they appropriate by faith—not only initially but continually—what happened in the death and resurrection of Christ. Another way of putting this is to say that "old" man refers to the old age in which man as incorporated in Adam is a slave to sin, whereas "new" man designates the new age in which man as a member of the body of Christ is now liberated from the slavery of sin and is free to live to the praise of God.

I believe that what Murray and Ridderbos are saying is of great significance for our subject. The old and the new man, it seems to me, ought not to be seen as aspects or sides or parts of the believer which are both still somehow present in him. How, then, should we understand these concepts? Murray can help us here. He says, " 'Old man' is a designation of the person in his unity as dominated by the flesh and sin" (p. 218). If this is so, it is obvious that the regenerated person is no longer an "old man." Paul says in Romans 6:6, "Knowing this, that our old man was crucified with him, that the body of sin might be done away, that so we should no longer be in bondage to sin"

(ASV). This crucifixion of the old man happened in salvation history. When Christ died on the cross, our old man —that is, our total person as enslaved by flesh and sin— was put to death with Him. This means that we who have been united with Christ through faith are no longer "old men." Our old man or old self has been put to death with Christ.

What happened when Christ was crucified, however, has also been subjectively appropriated by us. This is taught by Paul in the two other passages where the terms "old man" and "new man" occur: Ephesians 4:22-24 and Colossians 3:9-10. To quote just the latter passage, Paul there writes, "Lie not one to another; seeing that ye have put off the old man with his doings, and have put on the new man, that is being renewed unto knowledge after the image of him that created him" (ASV). After the analogy of what has just been said about the old man, we conclude that the new man must mean the person in his unity ruled by the Holy Spirit. In this passage, therefore, Paul appeals to his readers not to lie to each other because they have once and for all put off the old man or old self and have once and for all put on the new man or the new self.

Our self-image as Christians, therefore, must be of ourselves as those who have decisively rejected the old self or old man (the total person enslaved by sin), and have just as decisively appropriated the new self or the new man (the total person ruled by the Spirit). Because of what Christ has done for us, and because we, enabled by His Spirit, have grasped all His benefits by faith, we are now to look upon ourselves as no longer identified with the old self or old man, but as identified with the new self or the new man. We are to see ourselves, therefore, not as partly old selves and partly new selves, but as new persons in Christ.

Does this mean that for the believer the struggle against sin is over? No. The New Testament is full of the language of struggle: the Christian life is called a battle, a race, and a wrestling against evil spirits; we are told to be good Christian soldiers, to fight the good fight of the faith, to resist the devil, to take heed lest we fall, and to put on the whole armor of God. Moreover, in this struggle we do not always win, we do not resist every temptation. On the contrary, we hear New Testament saints confessing that they are far from perfection, that they have not yet attained, that in many things they all stumble. We hear John saying in his first epistle, "If we say we have no sin, we deceive ourselves and the truth is not in us" (1:8). The point is, however, that when we do fall into sin, we are momentarily living according to the old man, or the old self, which we have actually repudiated. We are then living contrary to what we really are in Christ. Though we are regenerate, we are then living contrary to our regenerate life. Though we have put on the new man, we are then living contrary to the new man, as if we were still the old man.

But the fact that this does happen—and may, indeed, happen frequently—does not mean that we must therefore revise our self-image as having to include both old man and new man. For—and this is a most important point— when we slip into an old-man way of living, we are living contrary to our true selves; we are denying our true self-image. Paul does not say in Romans 6:11, "Consider yourselves to be *mostly* alive to God and *mostly* dead to sin."

What he says is, "Consider yourselves dead to sin and alive to God." *This, then, must be our Christian self-image.* We must consider ourselves to be new persons in Christ, who have once and for all turned our backs upon the old self, and who therefore refuse to be identified with it any longer.

The old man or old self reveals itself in an old life-style, that of enslavement to sin. The new man or new self should reveal itself in a new life-style, that of joyful obedience to God. But it does not always do so. There are times when even the believer, who is a new person in Christ, lives in accordance with the old life-style. When he does so, however, he is being inconsistent with the person he truly is. Therefore Paul calls on believers to make their life-styles consistent with the new selves they have put on.

It might be well at this point to say something about the use of the word "depraved" as a term with which to describe believers. If it is true that the believer is to look upon himself as a new man in Christ, is it then proper to refer to such a person as still "depraved" or even as still "totally depraved"?

Perhaps a bit of historical background would be in order here. The concept of "total depravity" was developed by theologians in the Reformed or Calvinistic tradition to designate the condition of man as a fallen creature, apart from the regenerating and sanctifying influences of the Holy Spirit. The term was intended to convey two thoughts: (1) that in man as he is "by nature" the corruption or pollution of sin extends to every part of his being: to his mind as well as his appetites and impulses, to his aesthetic appreciation as well as his capacity to choose, and so on, and (2) that man in his natural state cannot do what is fundamentally pleasing to God, and cannot in his own strength change his basic preference for sin to love for God.

But now the question arises, is "depravity" or "total depravity" a proper expression to use in describing a regenerate man—a person to whom the Holy Spirit has given new spiritual life? We have just noted that the term was introduced to describe man apart from the regenerating and sanctifying work of the Spirit. That being the case, it should be obvious that the term ought not to be used to describe a person in whom the Spirit has begun the process of renewal and sanctification.

One might conceivably counter: But is it not true that even a regenerated person must still struggle against sin in every area of his life, in his thoughts as well as in his feelings, in his mind as well as in his appetites? Must not the believer still contend with the flesh, put to death the deeds of the body, and fight against indwelling sin? Indeed he must. But since the believer is now in Christ, indwelt by the Holy Spirit, he has been endowed with power to resist temptation and to overcome sin—a power which the unregenerate man does not have.

For these reasons I conclude that one ought not to say that a regenerate person is still "totally depraved." Though the believer is still inclined to all kinds of sin, the indwelling Spirit now enables him more and more to say no to sin. We ought therefore to see him, think of him, and describe him as a person who is a new creature in Christ, who is being progressively renewed in the image of God.

CHAPTER FOUR

Life in the Spirit

The Christian is to see himself as a new man in Christ, who has been delivered from the enslavement to sin called the "old man." His image of himself, therefore, must be primarily positive, not negative. Let us now go on to see what the New Testament teaches us about life in the Spirit.

There is a close connection between being a new man in Christ and living in the Spirit. This will become evident as we go from Romans 6 to Romans 8. In Romans 6:6 Paul describes the Christian as a person whose "old man" was crucified with Christ, so that he is no longer enslaved to sin. In Romans 8:2 and 9, however, he depicts that same person as someone whom the Spirit of life in Christ Jesus has set free from the law of sin and death, and as someone who is no longer in the flesh but in the Spirit.

What does Paul mean by "flesh" and "Spirit"? We must not see in these two concepts a contrast between two aspects of man's nature, a "fleshly" aspect and a "spiritual" one. We must rather see in these terms a description of two contrasting power-spheres associated with the two ages distinguished from each other through the coming of Jesus

Christ. Let us say that apart from the coming of Christ man is by nature under the domination of the flesh. This refers, it should be emphasized, not to man's physical nature but to his whole being as it is under the power of sin. But when Christ came, He ushered in a new way of living which is called life in the Spirit. To be in the Spirit means that people who were formerly under the sway of the flesh as a sinful power have now been brought under the liberating regime of the Spirit (Ridderbos, *Paul,* p. 221).

In the New Testament Christians are sometimes said to be "in the Spirit," but at other times they are described as those who walk "according to the Spirit" (Rom. 8:4) or "by the Spirit" (Gal. 5:16 and 25). Elsewhere in Paul's writings believers are designated as people who are "led by the Spirit" (Rom. 8:14), "sealed with the Spirit" (Eph. 1:13), or as those who ought to be "filled with the Spirit" (Eph. 5:18). All of these descriptions again imply a positive self-image: the believer should look upon himself as no longer a slave of the flesh but as free in the Spirit.

In the last chapter we noted that as long as the Christian is in this life he must continue to fight against sin. We also saw, however, that this fact need not imply a negative self-image. We now take another look at this lifelong battle, this time in terms of the struggle between flesh and Spirit.

In Galatians 5:16 Paul says, "But I say, Walk by the Spirit, and ye shall not fulfil the lust of the flesh" (ASV). The Revised Standard Version here is mistaken when it translates the second half of the verse as if it were a second command: "and do not gratify the desires of the flesh." In the original Greek the second clause is not a prohibition but a strong negation; it really amounts to a promise: If you walk by the Spirit, you shall not in any way fulfil the lust of the flesh. As we saw above, "flesh" here is to be understood not as referring to man's physical body, but as designating his total nature when it is under the domination or enslavement of sin. As the power of the flesh reveals itself in behavior, it stands for a sinful way of living and is therefore similar in meaning to the Pauline concept of the "old man."

"Spirit" here probably means the Holy Spirit, though there are some who interpret the word as referring to the "new nature" which was bestowed at the time of regeneration. The fact that the struggle in the Christian is here described as one between the Holy Spirit and the flesh implies that believers must still do battle against fleshly impulses. But this does not mean that believers are still "in the flesh" in the sense of "enslaved by the flesh." The plain teaching of the passage is that, since believers are now under the rule and power of the Holy Spirit, they can triumph over the desires of the flesh and are no longer enslaved by it. Paul puts this very clearly in Romans 8:9, "But you are not in the flesh; you are in the Spirit."

Getting back now to Galatians, in 5:17 Paul says, "For the desires of the flesh are against the Spirit, and the desires of the Spirit are against the flesh; for these are opposed to each other, to prevent you from doing what you would." The last clause, "to prevent you from doing what you would," is often interpreted as meaning, "to prevent you from doing the good which you want to do." In this interpretation the flesh is understood to be so powerful in the life of the Christian that it prevents him from doing the good things he really wants to do. The trouble with this interpretation, however, is that it represents an abrupt shift from the mood of victory to that of defeat. In actual fact, verse 17 gives a reason for the triumphant statement of verse 16, which is, "Walk by the Spirit, and you shall not fulfil the desires of the flesh." Why is this so? Because, so Paul says in verse 17, these two are contrary to each other: "the desires of the flesh are against the Spirit, and the desires of the Spirit are against the flesh." This being the case, it follows that if you walk by the Spirit you will not continue doing the bad things you might otherwise be inclined to do. The atmosphere of the passage is not one of defeat but of victory!

There follows a listing of the works of the flesh, and a warning that those who do such things shall not inherit the kingdom of God. Then comes the well-known description of the fruit of the Spirit: "But the fruit of the Spirit is love, joy, peace, patience, kindness, goodness, faithfulness, gentleness, self-control" (vv. 22-23). The interesting thing is that although the *works* of the flesh are many, the *fruit* of the Spirit is one. The implication would seem to be that if one grows in one of the aspects of the fruit—say, love—he will also grow in the other aspects. If we keep on walking by the Spirit, we shall keep on abounding in the fruit of the Spirit.

We come now to verse 24, where Paul sums up once again what it means to be a Christian: "And those who belong to Christ Jesus have crucified the flesh with its passions and desires." The Christian, so Paul teaches us here, is a person who has once and for all turned his back upon the flesh and all the works associated with the flesh, and is now walking by the Spirit. It is therefore not correct to say that the Christian is part flesh and part Spirit. He is in the Spirit, and has decisively repudiated the way of living called the flesh. When he does "gratify the desires of the flesh," he is going contrary to what he really is.

So we see again that the Christian's self-image is to be a positive one: the believer is to look upon himself as someone who is in Christ and in the Spirit, and is no longer in the flesh. The fact that he may sometimes give way to the flesh does not mean that he must modify his self-image to leave room for such defections. In such instances the Christian is "not really himself," is acting contrary to his true purpose.

This is not to deny that there continue to be struggle and tension in the Christian life. But the unique message of the New Testament is this: For those who are in Christ, and therefore in the Spirit, the battle against sin is to be fought in an atmosphere of victory, not defeat. "Walk by the Spirit," Paul says, "and you shall not fulfil the lust of the flesh."

Ridderbos sums up Paul's outlook as follows: "The dominant viewpoint under which Paul views the Christian life is not the continuing onslaught of the flesh on the believer, but the power of the Spirit which enables him to win the victory over sin" (*Paul,* p. 272). Our way of viewing ourselves should reflect this kind of victorious faith. In our self-image, as well as in other areas of life, we must not be overcome by evil, but must overcome evil with good.

CHAPTER FIVE
The New Creature

How are we to view ourselves? As we continue to ask what the Bible teaches us about the Christian self-image, let us see what light is shed on this question by the Scriptural concept of the new creation.

The passage which springs to mind at once in this connection is II Corinthians 5:17: "Therefore, if any one is in Christ, he is a new creation; the old has passed away, behold, the new has come." It will be noted that translations vary in the way they render the Greek word *ktisis* here: some have "creation," while others have "creature."

The primary meaning of the passage is probably this: The person who is in Christ is to be seen as a member of God's new creation, as someone who belongs to the new age which was ushered in by Christ. Note the contrast between old and new: the old era of enslavement to sin is gone, and the new era of salvation, freedom, and joy inaugurated by Christ's resurrection has come. Everyone who is in Christ, therefore, now belongs to this new world.

Lewis Smedes, in his study of union with Christ entitled *All Things Made New,* also sees this passage in a salvation-history context: because of Christ's reconciling work a new creation has come into existence, and all who are in Christ now have a part in that new creation (pp. 104-108). In what is perhaps the finest passage in his book he goes on to say,

> The familiar text about being "new creatures in Christ" should not be waved too easily as a slogan for what happens "in me" when I am converted. The design of Christ's new creation is far too grand, too inclusive to be restricted to what happens inside my soul. No nook or cranny of history is too small for its purpose, no cultural potential too large for its embrace. Being in Christ, we are part of a new movement by His grace, a movement rolling on toward the new heaven and new earth where all things are made right and where He is all in all. (pp. 127-28)

With all this I would agree. Yet I believe that II Corinthians 5:17 also has much to say about our Christian self-image. Since believers now belong to Christ's new creation, we are to see ourselves as new creatures in Christ, not just as depraved sinners. To be sure, apart from Christ we are sinners, but we are no longer apart from Christ. In Christ we are now justified sinners, sinners who have the Holy Spirit dwelling within, sinners who are being progressively renewed. Our way of looking at ourselves must not deny this newness but affirm it.

We must understand, in other words, that the Christian life involves not just believing something about Christ, but also believing something about ourselves. The something we are to believe about ourselves is that we are now in Christ, part of His new creation and therefore in a very real sense new creatures. To be sure, we are not yet totally new creatures; we do continue to slide into old ways of thinking and living, and we are not yet what we shall be.

Yet Paul says, "If any one is in Christ, he *is* a new creation" (or a new creature) already here and now. Our faith in Christ must include believing that we are exactly what the Bible says we are.

If we turn now to Galatians 2:20, we shall note that Paul there says, "I have been crucified with Christ; it is no longer I that live, but Christ who lives in me; and the life I now live in the flesh I live by faith. . . ." These words imply that we can keep on grasping the fact that Christ lives in us only by continuing to exercise faith. Having a proper Christian self-image, therefore, is an aspect of our Christian faith. Conversely, failing to see ourselves as new creatures in Christ is tantamount to a denial of our faith.

This is a good point at which to consider a problem many people have with the cultivation of a positive self-image. The problem is this: How can one have a positive self-image and still avoid spiritual pride? Will not such a self-image bring with it a kind of holier-than-thou attitude? Will it not lead a person to think of himself as superior to others?

The Bible warns us sharply against such thinking. Jesus' words are well known: "Whoever exalts himself will be humbled, and whoever humbles himself will be exalted" (Matt. 23:12). Paul warns us not to think of ourselves more highly than we ought to think (Rom. 12:3), and Peter says, "God opposes the proud but gives grace to the humble" (I Pet. 5:5).

How, then, can one have a positive self-image and still avoid this kind of pride? The answer is to be found in a proper understanding of the Christian self-image. The Christian is not to think of himself *apart from Christ* as someone worthy of high esteem. But the image the

Christian should have of himself is of someone who is *in Christ* and is *therefore* a new creature. The proper Christian self-image, in other words, does not imply pride in ourselves but rather glorying in what Christ has done for us and continues to do for us.

It will be recalled that this was precisely the case with the Apostle Paul. Though he calls himself the chief of sinners and the least of all the saints, he yet says, "By the grace of God I am what I am" (I Cor. 15:10). He claims that his sufficiency is not in himself but only in God (II Cor. 3:5). His boasting is in the Lord rather than in himself; as far as his own person is concerned, he boasts of his weaknesses, so that the power of Christ may fully rest upon him (II Cor. 12:9). Paul's positive self-image, therefore, is not an evidence of spiritual pride, but rather a fruit of his faith in Christ.

This brings us back to the point at which this little digression about the danger of spiritual pride began. As was said before, having a proper Christian self-image is an aspect of our Christian faith. The main burden of this book is not a plea for believers to have an exalted opinion of themselves; it is rather a plea to Christians to see themselves through the eyes of faith.

We would all, I am sure, be very critical of a believer who stopped looking at Jesus Christ through the eyes of faith and began to think of Him either as a mistaken man who entertained delusions of grandeur about Himself and His mission, or as a mere teacher of morality. We would insist—and rightly so—that we can properly understand Jesus Christ only if we see Him as the Scriptures teach us to see Him: as the God-man, the Word made flesh, who came to earth to save us from our sins. Why not, then, apply the same kind of thinking to the question of our self-image? Why should we not be equally critical of a believer who has stopped looking at himself through the eyes of faith, and who therefore sees himself as only a miserable sinner? Why should we not insist with equal fervor that we can only truly understand ourselves when we see ourselves as the Scriptures teach us to do: unworthy mortals who have been redeemed from sin, and who have therefore been made new creatures, indwelt by Jesus Christ, temples of the Holy Spirit?

The Christian self-image, when properly understood, is the very opposite of spiritual pride. It goes hand in hand with a deep conviction of sin and a recognition that we are unworthy of the least of God's blessings. It means glorying not in self but in Christ.

We have been thinking so far in this chapter about the Christian as a new creature. But what would be the point of calling ourselves new creatures if doing so made no difference whatever in our daily lives? Being a new creature does indeed involve a new way of living. This new way of living is variously described in the New Testament as living no longer for self but for Christ (II Cor. 5:15), as presenting ourselves to God as living sacrifices (Rom. 12:1), as being transformed by the renewal of our minds (Rom. 12:2), and as a life of victory over sin (I John 5:4).

That the Bible describes the Christian life as a life of victory will be evident as we look at a few illustrative passages. In Romans 6:14 Paul teaches that because we are no longer under law but under grace, sin shall no longer be our master (NEB). In Romans 8:2 he affirms that the law (here probably best understood as the *power*) of the

Spirit of life in Christ Jesus has set us free from the law
(read *power* again) of sin and death. And in Romans 8:37
he shouts triumphantly. "In all these things we are more
than conquerors through him who loved us." In the light of
passages of this sort, for a Christian to have an image of
himself as someone who is constantly being defeated by
sin or adversity is to entertain a self-image which contra-
dicts Scripture. And for people who say, with a nonchalant
shrug of the shoulders, "Well, we really can't help sinning,
you know," there is always I Corinthians 10:13: "No
temptation has overtaken you that is not common to man.
God is faithful, and he will not let you be tempted beyond
your strength, but with the temptation will also provide
the way of escape, that you may be able to endure it."

We have already noted the victory motif in Galatians
5:16-25. Though the Christian must still struggle against
the flesh, he knows that in the strength of the Spirit he
can be victorious. The well-known words of Philippians
4:13 were originally uttered in connection with the question of contentment; yet they have a bearing, I believe, on
the possibility of victorious living: "I can do all things
in him who strengthens me." And John certainly sounds
the note of victory in his first epistle, chapter 5:4, when
he says, "For whatever is born of God overcomes the
world; and this is the victory that overcomes the world,
our faith." As those who have that faith, we must see ourselves not as victims but as victors.

All this is not to say that the Bible teaches the possibility
of attaining sinless perfection in this life. This point will
be taken up in greater detail in a later chapter. At this
stage let it simply be said that the Scriptures do not per-
mit us to take such a position. Though we look forward to

the realization of sinless perfection in the life to come, in this present life we shall never get beyond the need for daily confession of sin, as Christ Himself taught us in the fifth petition of the Lord's Prayer.

But what the Bible does teach us is that we who are in Christ are to view ourselves as new creatures who are now in the strength of His Spirit living a life of victory. It is in such terms that the New Testament describes the Christian. Granted, the believer may lose many a battle, particularly when he relies on his own strength instead of looking to the Lord. But one may lose many battles and still win the war. And when one is in Christ the final outcome is never in question.

CHAPTER SIX

Romans Seven

We have seen that the New Testament teaches the believer to look at himself as a new man who has been delivered from the slavery of sin, as a new creature, as someone who is more than a conqueror through Christ who loves him.

All this sounds very good, someone might say at this point, but how about Romans 7? Doesn't Paul in this chapter teach us that even we who are Christians don't do the good we want to do, and do the evil we don't want to do? Doesn't he tell us that although we can will what is right, we cannot do it? Doesn't he assure us that although we may indeed delight in the law of God in our inmost self, there is another law in our members which makes us captives of sin? If this chapter describes the Christian believer, how can such a constantly frustrated person have a positive self-image? How can he see himself as a victor in Christ when he finds himself repeatedly defeated by sin? How can he view himself as a new creature when there is still so much of the old in him?

The problem here concerns particularly the interpretation

of Romans 7:13-25. Does this passage describe the situation of the regenerate person? Do these words give us a picture of the struggle against sin which takes place in the daily life of every believer? Is this passage a description of the normal Christian life?

It must be granted that a great many interpreters, both past and present, so understand these words. But it should also be said that there are a number of evangelical scholars who hold to a different understanding of the passage.

I believe that what we have here in Romans 7:13-25 is not a description of the regenerate man, but of the unregenerate man who is trying to fight sin through the law alone, apart from the strength of the Holy Spirit. I grant that this is a picture of the unregenerate man seen through the eyes of a regenerate man, since Paul wrote these words after his conversion. This fact helps us to understand the vivid and perceptive way in which sin is here described. But it is the struggle of the unregenerate man (or the regenerate man when he tries to "go it alone") that is here depicted, not the normal life of the believer.

My reasons for interpreting the passage this way are as follows:

(1) Romans 7:13-25 reflects and elaborates on the condition pictured in 7:5. In 7:4 we read, "Likewise, my brethren, you have died to the law through the body of Christ, so that you may belong to another, to him who has been raised from the dead in order that we may bear fruit for God." You believers, Paul is saying, died to the law because you were crucified with Christ; since you are one with Christ not only in His death but also in His resurrection, you have now been made to belong to Christ—you have been married to Christ, so to speak—so that you might bear fruit for

God. In the next verse, however (v. 5), Paul goes on to say, "While we were living in the flesh, our sinful passions, aroused by the law, were at work in our members to bear fruit for death." Obviously what is here being described is a state previous to conversion, when we believers were still "living in the flesh." At that time we were not keeping the law, but rather found that the law aroused our sinful passions; as a result, we were then bringing forth fruit not for God, but for death.

If we may for the moment skip over verse 6, we shall see that the condition described in verse 5 is precisely the condition reflected in Romans 7:13-25. Verse 13 sums up the situation pictured in verse 5: "Did that which is good, then, bring death to me? By no means! It was sin, working death in me through what is good, in order that sin might be shown to be sin, and through the commandment might become sinful beyond measure." Verse 14, which follows, begins with the word "for" (unfortunately omitted in the Revised Standard Version): "For we know that the law is spiritual; but I am carnal, sold under sin." It is important also to observe that the Greek text of the next verse contains two "for"s, only one of which is reproduced in the Revised Standard Version: "For I do not understand my own actions. For I do not do what I want, but I do the very thing I hate." By means of these "for"s Paul is tying in what follows with what he has said before. The rest of chapter 7 is thus an elaboration of the condition described in verse 5. It will be recalled that the condition described in verse 5 is a state prior to conversion, when the people pictured in that verse were still "living in the flesh."

(2) One finds no mention of the Holy Spirit or of the strength He provides for overcoming sin in Romans 7:13-

25, whereas there are at least sixteen references to the Holy Spirit in chapter 8. This fact cannot be without significance.

(3) The mood of frustration and defeat which permeates Romans 7:13-25 does not comport with the mood of victory in terms of which Paul usually describes the normal life of the Christian. We have already noted that in Galatians 5:16-25 Paul depicts the Christian struggle as between flesh and Spirit—but in an atmosphere of victory, not defeat. When Paul says, for instance, in Romans 7:23 that he sees in his members another law at war with the law of his mind, making him captive to the law of sin which dwells in his members, he certainly does not seem to be picturing the same situation as that which he describes in Romans 8:2: "For the law of the Spirit of life in Christ Jesus has set me free from the law of sin and death."

(4) Many commentators have called attention to the unusual words found in Romans 7:25, "So then, I of myself serve the law of God with my mind, but with my flesh I serve the law of sin." The words "of myself" are emphatic. They suggest that Paul is indeed describing a person who tries to "go it himself" or "go it alone"—to live the obedient life in his own strength, instead of in the strength of the Spirit.

(5) As I have already suggested, there is an abrupt change of mood as we go from Romans 7 to Romans 8. Romans 8:2 tells us how we have obtained freedom from the "law of sin and death": "For the law of the Spirit of life in Christ Jesus has set me free from the law of sin and death." Paul uses the word "law" in various ways in his writings; in the verse just quoted he uses law in the sense of "principle" or "power." The power of the Spirit, he says, has set me free from the power of sin and death.

This power of sin and death is what he has been experiencing during his unregenerate state. It is precisely the workings of this "law of sin and death" which have been described in such lurid colors in the second half of Romans 7 (note how often the very words "sin" and "death" occur in that passage). But now, Paul says triumphantly in 8:2, by the power of the Spirit of life in Christ Jesus, I and all believers with me have been set free from the slavery of sin and death!

What Paul says in 8:2, therefore, is actually a restatement of what he had said in 7:6, "But now we are discharged from the law, dead to that which held us captive, so that we serve not under the old written code but in the new life of the Spirit." These words obviously describe, not the unregenerate man who is still "living in the flesh," but the regenerate man who has been delivered from the slavery of sin. The rest of chapter 7, beginning with the seventh verse, is an elaboration of the unregenerate condition pictured in verse 5. One could say, therefore, that 7:7-25 constitutes a kind of interlude, elaborating on and vividly dramatizing the condition pictured in 7:5, but that chapter 8 goes back to 7:6 and expands upon the state set forth there——that of the regenerate man.

(6) Romans 8:4 teaches us that the reason why God sent His Son into the world is "that the just requirement of the law might be fulfilled in us, who walk not according to the flesh but according to the Spirit." These words do not expound the fact that Christ has kept the law *for* us (for in that case the preposition before "us" would have to be something other than "in"), but they affirm that God sent His Son so that the requirement of the law might be fulfilled *in* us or *by* us. This passage, further, does not speak

only of what will be the case in the life to come; it obviously has a present reference. This being so, we must conclude
that believers are not doomed to perpetual defeat in trying
to keep the law—the kind of defeat pictured in Romans
7—but are now able to fulfil the law's just requirement, in
principle though not yet in perfection, through the indwelling Spirit who enables and strengthens them.

What we have, therefore, in Romans 7:13-25 is a vivid
description of the inability of a person to do what is pleasing to God in his own strength with only the law to help
him. This description would strike home to the Jews among
Paul's readers who set great stock by the law and thought
the way to the good life was to be found through keeping
the law. Such an effort, Paul is saying here, can only lead to
perpetual frustration! It would also be possible, I agree, for
a regenerate Christian to slip into the type of life described
in the latter half of Romans 7, if he stopped walking by
the Spirit and tried to keep the law of God in his own
strength. But I do not believe, for the reasons given above,
that the passage in question describes the typical life-style
of the regenerate believer.

The interpretation of Romans 7 given above has important implications for our view of the Christian self-
image. To understand the passage in this way does not imply that there is no struggle against sin in the Christian
life; it only implies that Romans 7:13-25 does not describe
that struggle in its usual form. I do not believe it is proper, for example, for a Christian who has fallen into some
sin to quote from this passage as a kind of "excuse" for his
lapse. I do not think it is a responsible use of the chapter
for a believer to say, "It's no wonder I fall so far short of
what I ought to be, for even that great saint, the Apostle

Paul, had to confess, 'I do not do the good I want, but the evil I do not want is what I do.' "

Understanding Romans 7:13-25 in the way described above will help us come to greater clarity on the question of the Christian's self-image. There is struggle in the Christian life, to be sure, but the struggle is to be carried on, not in an atmosphere of constant defeat, but in an atmosphere of victory. The person described in the second half of Romans 7 seems doomed to perpetual frustration; he is continually hitting his head against the wall. But the person described in Romans 8 is one who, strengthened by the Spirit, is fulfilling the just requirement of the law, is putting to death the deeds of the body, is setting his mind on the things of the Spirit, and is therefore more than a conqueror through the One who loved him. It is Romans 8, not Romans 7, which pictures what the normal Christian life is like. Accordingly, the biblical view of the Christian's self-image is to be drawn, not from Romans 7, but from Romans 8.

CHAPTER SEVEN

Sinless Perfection?

Does having a positive self-image imply that we are able in this present life to live without sin? Let us see what the Bible teaches us about this question.

There is a passage in John's first epistle which is often quoted as proof that sinless perfection here and now is indeed possible for those who have been born again. The passage reads as follows: "No one born of God commits sin; for God's nature abides in him, and he cannot sin because he is born of God" (I John 3:9). At first glance this text does seem to teach not only the possibility but even the likelihood that those who have been "born of God" will no longer commit any sin.

But in order to understand fully what John is saying here, we must first look carefully at some other passages from his first epistle. Note, for example, what he says in 1:8: "If we say that we have no sin, we deceive ourselves, and the truth is not in us." In the next verse John clearly implies that believers must still confess their sins: "If we confess our sins, he is faithful and just, and will forgive our sins and cleanse us from all unrighteousness." The need for repeated confession on the part of believers rules out the possibility of their living without sin. To the same effect are the words of 2:1: "My little children, I am writing this to you so that you may not sin; but if anyone does sin, we have an advocate with the Father, Jesus Christ the righteous." If John believed that the Christians to whom he was writing were no longer capable of committing any sin, he would certainly not have written the second half of this verse.

These verses clearly teach that any Christian who claims that he has no sin whatever, and that he no longer needs to confess his sins, is deceiving himself. Obviously, then, when John says in 3:9 that "no one born of God commits sin," he does not mean that the regenerate person is able here and now to live a life which is completely free from sin.

How, then, are we to interpret this puzzling remark? To understand it properly, we need to look carefully at the tenses John is using. In this passage the tenses that are used to describe the kind of sinning which the regenerate person does not and cannot do are present, and the present tense in Greek indicates continued or habitual action. Literally translated, this verse would read, "No one who has been born of God continually lives in sin . . . and he is not able to keep on living in sin because he has been born of God." What this passage teaches, therefore, is that the regenerate person cannot and does not continue to live in sin.

In 2:1, however, the tenses used to describe the kind of sinning which a regenerate person can still do are aorists, and aorists in Greek commonly indicate snapshot action, momentary action. A literal translation of this verse, therefore, might read somewhat as follows: "My little children, I write these things to you so that you may not commit sin. And if any one does commit a sin, we have an advocate with the Father." What John is here teaching us is that a regenerate person (for he is writing to believers) can still fall into sin, but that when he does so he should not despair, since he has an Advocate with the Father through whom he may obtain forgiveness. Putting all these passages together, we find John saying something like this: The regenerate person may still *fall* into sin, but he cannot *live* in sin. John Stott, in his Tyndale Commentary on the Epistles of John, puts it this way: ". . . The sin a Christian 'does not' and 'cannot' do is habitual and persistent sin." And he quotes David Smith as saying, "The believer may fall into sin, but he will not walk in it" (pp. 135-36).

Other Scripture passages may be adduced, from both Old and New Testaments, which also rule out the possibility of sinless perfection in this life. In I Kings 8:46 we read, "For there is no man who does not sin." The words of Isaiah 53:6 are well known: "All we like sheep have gone astray; we have turned every one to his own way." Paul says in Romans 3:23, "All have sinned and fall short of the glory of God." James says, "For in many things we all stumble" (3:2, ASV). And in a prayer which was intended to be offered daily, our Lord taught us to pray, "Forgive us our sins, for we ourselves forgive every one who is indebted to us" (Luke 11:4).

We must realize that as long as we live on this side of the Second Coming of Christ we live in a kind of tension between what we now are and what we shall some day become. The Bible teaches that in the life to come, when the process of redemption shall have reached its goal, we shall be able to live in sinless perfection. But such sinless perfection is unattainable as long as we are in this present life. And therefore we live in a kind of tension between what we now have and what we shall have, between the "already" and the "not-yet."

Many recent theologians have written about this tension in the Christian life. Oscar Cullmann, in his *Christ and Time,* has given us an interesting analogy of this tension. Referring to terms familiar from World War II, Cullmann suggests that we who are Christians live between D-day and V-day. D-day was the decisive battle of World War II, but the enemy did not lay down their arms until V-day. So for us, though our spiritual enemies have been decisively defeated by Jesus Christ, there remain pockets of resistance here and there, there are still battles to be fought, there are still guerilla troops to be reduced to submission. Satan knows that he has been defeated; yet he keeps fighting on. In one sense we already possess salvation, but in another sense we still look forward to our salvation. We *already* have the new life; we do *not yet* have perfection.

Paul often gives expression to this tension. Though he teaches that Christ has defeated Satan, he tells his readers at Ephesus to "put on the whole armor of God, that you may be able to stand against the wiles of the devil" (Eph. 6:11). Whereas he affirms repeatedly that in the power of the Spirit believers can resist temptation, he warns his Corinthian readers, "Let any one who thinks that he stands take heed lest he fall" (I Cor. 10:12). The fact that Christ has won the victory for us does not take away the need for constant watchfulness and soberness, lest we fall into sinful ways of thinking or living.

Paul sees the Christian life as something of surpassing

worth, but also as something which is destined to become even more beautiful in the future. In Philippians 3:7 he writes, "Whatever gain I had, I counted as loss for the sake of Christ. Indeed, I count everything as loss because of the surpassing worth of knowing Christ Jesus my Lord." What he is saying here is this: What I now have in Christ is so tremendous that I have willingly given up everything that was gain to me so that I might have this great benefit. Yet a few verses further on he says, "Not that I have already obtained this [the resurrection from the dead] or am already perfect; but I press on to make it my own. . . . Brethren, I do not consider that I have made it my own; but one thing I do, forgetting what lies behind and straining forward to what lies ahead, I press on toward the goal . . ." (vv. 12-14). Probably the most triumphant chapter in the Bible is Romans 8; yet even in this chapter, which so jubilantly celebrates the present victory of the Christian over the powers of sin and death, Paul has to say, in verse 23, "And not only the creation, but we ourselves, who have the first fruits of the Spirit, groan inwardly as we wait for adoption as sons, the redemption of our bodies."

Our self-image, then, must be seen in the light of this tension between the already and the not-yet. We are in Christ, to be sure, and therefore we share in His decisive victory over the powers of evil. But, since we are still on this side of His Second Coming, we do not yet enjoy the totality of Christ's victory. Our self-image must leave room for the future—for the fact that we are not yet what we shall be. What we have here and now is only the beginning, only the first-fruits. The best is yet to come! C. S. Lewis has put it unforgettably: "All your life an unattainable ecstasy has hovered just beyond the grasp of your consciousness. The day is coming when you will wake to find, beyond all hope, that you have attained it . . ." (*The Problem of Pain*, p. 136).

Though this is so, it remains true that our self-image should be primarily positive, not negative. For the eschatological outlook of the Bible is not this: "You are in bad shape now, but cheer up! Things will be much better by and by." Rather, it is this: "If you are in Christ, you already are fabulously rich. But some day you shall be infinitely richer!" When the New Testament describes the Christian, it emphasizes, not the continued sinfulness of the believer, but his newness in Christ. Our self-image ought to reflect that emphasis.

In this connection we should look at another biblical concept describing the person who is being redeemed: that of progressive transformation. The Bible pictures believers as people who are progressing toward the goal, who are "growing up into Christ" (Eph. 4:15), who are being "renewed in the spirit of their minds" (Eph. 4:23). This being the case, our self-image must not be static but dynamic. We may never be satisfied with ourselves, but must always be pressing on toward the goal of Christian perfection.

Though, as we have seen, we are to think of ourselves as new persons in Christ, the new man which we have put on, so Paul reminds us in Colossians 3:10, is being continually renewed in knowledge after the image of its Creator. It is interesting to note that in the Greek text of verses 9 and 10 there is variation in the tenses of the verbs used: "Lie not one to another; seeing that ye have put off (aorist) the old man with his doings, and have put on (aorist) the new man, that is being renewed (present) unto knowledge after the image of him that created him" (ASV). Since the aorist tense in Greek describes "snapshot" action and the present tense continuing action, we could paraphrase the verse as follows: "Do not lie to one another, seeing that you have put off, once and for all, the old man . . . and have put on, once and for all, the new man which is being continually renewed in knowledge. . . ." What Paul is saying here, in other words, is that the new man which we put on at the time of our conversion is being progressively renewed. "New man" is not a static concept but a dynamic one: it points to a new self which is not yet perfect but is continually being renewed.

To the same effect is a passage from what is often called a twin epistle to Colossians, Ephesians 4:22-24. With John Murray (*Principles of Conduct,* pp. 214-19), I prefer to think of the verbs here as meaning "this is how you *did* learn Christ," rather than "this is how you *must* learn Christ." As in the Colossians text, the verb forms vary from aorist to present and then back to aorist again. We could paraphrase as follows, beginning with verse 20: "You did not so learn Christ . . . seeing that you have put off, once and for all, your old man . . . are being continually renewed in the spirit of your minds, and have put on, once and for all, the new man. . . ." Again we have here a fascinating interplay between the once-for-all and the progressive aspect of the Christian life. When you became believers, Paul is saying to the Ephesians, you burned your bridges behind you: you decisively put off your old man and with equal decisiveness put on the new. At the same time, however, there is a continuing process going on in your lives: you are being progressively renewed in the spirit of your minds.

This progressive renewal involves our own responsible activity. Paul teaches this in II Corinthians 7:1: "Having therefore these promises, beloved, let us cleanse ourselves from all defilement of flesh and spirit, perfecting holiness in the fear of God" (ASV). The expression "perfecting holiness" literally means "bringing holiness to its goal." The same point is made in Romans 12:2: "Do not be conformed to this world but be transformed by the renewal of your mind. . . ." "Be transformed" is in the present tense, meaning "be continually, progressively transformed." The word "transformed" points not just to outward change but to inner transformation: new motives, new values, new goals. This is our continuing challenge.

At the same time, however, this renewal is God's work within us. Whereas in Romans 12:2 Paul views our continuing transformation as the task of the believer, in II Corinthians 3:18 he affirms that this transformation is wrought in us by the Holy Spirit: "And we all, with unveiled face, reflecting (using the marginal translation here) the glory of the Lord, are being changed into his likeness from one degree of glory to another; for this comes from the Lord who is the Spirit."

The passage reminds us that this progressive transformation is actually the restoration of the image of God within us. From the first chapter of Genesis we learn that God made man in His own image. When man fell into sin, that image became corrupted and distorted. When God redeems us from sin, His purpose is to restore His image in us. Accordingly, the new life in us is described in Colossians 3:10 as the putting on of the new man which is being renewed in knowledge after the image of its Creator. Since Christ is the image of the invisible God (Col. 1:15), the

New Testament can also describe the goal of redemption as that of bringing us into conformity with the image of God's Son (Rom. 8:29), and of changing us more and more into the likeness of the Lord Jesus Christ (II Cor. 3:18). We are therefore to see ourselves as being progressively transformed into the image of Christ, thus becoming more and more like God.

This process will be brought to its goal only in the life to come. But it is certain to be finished, since the God who has begun a good work in us will bring it to completion at the day of Jesus Christ (Phil. 1:6). Already now we are new creatures in Christ. Some day that newness will be complete. "Beloved, we are God's children now; it does not yet appear what we shall be, but we know that when he appears we shall be like him, for we shall see him as he is" (I John 3:2).

Chapter Eight

Christian Acceptance

So far we have seen that the Bible teaches us to have positive images of ourselves, to see ourselves as new creatures in Christ rather than as impotent and depraved sinners. Let us now go on to explore the implications of this teaching for our relations to and dealings with others, particularly with fellow Christians.

There is, in fact, an obvious connection between a negative self-image and a critical attitude toward others. The person who is always running other people down is very likely trying to bolster his own ego because his self-image is poor. This procedure is particularly satisfying to a person with a negative self-image because as long as he is criticizing the other person, he does not need to be too concerned about his own shortcomings.

Conversely, in order to be properly appreciative of other people, we need a positive image of ourselves. It is only when I can forget about myself and my own ego that I can be free to appreciate and honor others. When, for example, Paul tells us in Philippians 2:3 that in lowliness of mind we are to count others better than ourselves, he does not imply that we must demean ourselves or think of ourselves as inferior to others. The point is rather that we must not seek our own honor at someone else's expense, and that we must be more concerned to honor and praise others than we are to have others praise us. J. B. Phillips has, I believe, effectively captured the spirit of this verse when he translates, "Never act from motives of rivalry or personal vanity, but in humility think more of one another than you do of yourselves." One is also reminded of Romans 12:10, where Paul counsels his readers to "outdo one another in showing honor."

What this means is that we must be more eager to see others get honor than we are to be honored ourselves. But this does not imply that we need to despise ourselves or to deprecate ourselves. As a matter of fact, it requires a pretty healthy kind of self-esteem for us to be more concerned for the other man's honor than for our own. In order to be free to give to others the honor which is their due, we must be willing to leave the matter of our own vindication or recognition completely in the Lord's hands.

We have been developing the point that according to biblical teaching we are to see ourselves as those who are in Christ and therefore new creatures. But in the New Testament the concept of being in Christ is never thought of in individualistic terms. It is not just an individual here and there who is in Christ; it is Christ's people who are in Him. He is the vine and they are the branches; He is the head and they are the body. Because this is so, we who are in Christ are not only members of Christ but also members of each other (Rom. 12:4-5).

It follows that we are to see not just ourselves as being in Christ, but also our fellow Christians. We must understand this matter of being in Christ not just in individual but also in social dimensions. All of us who are Christians are in Christ together. In this chapter and in the next we shall be looking at some of the implications of this "being-in-Christ-together" for our Christian life-style.

One of the most important implications is that of accepting one another. Counselors and psychotherapists tell us that acceptance is one of the most basic prerequisites for good counseling—so much so that if the person counseled does not feel that the counselor totally accepts him just as he is, no effective counseling will be possible. It should now be observed that the concept of acceptance is also an important biblical principle.

In Romans 15:7 Paul tells us, "In a word, accept one another as Christ accepted us, to the glory of God" (NEB). Other versions translate the Greek verb used here as "receive" or "welcome," but I believe "accept" is as good a rendering as any. These words, occurring in the middle of a discussion of the relationship between "strong" and "weak" Christians, suggest that accepting fellow Christians is a primary Christian duty. Whether a fellow Christian be "weak" or "strong," whether he believes he may eat anything or only vegetables, whether he is the kind of person to whom we are naturally attracted or whether he is rather unattractive, we must accept him.

It is important to note that we are told here to accept one another as Christ has accepted us. The word "as" in this passage may be construed as meaning both "because" and "in the same manner." We are to accept one another first of all *because* Christ has accepted us. Failure to accept a fellow Christian reveals a lack of gratitude for Christ's acceptance of us, whereas if we accept our Christian brothers we show

how thankful we are for the priceless blessing of our salvation. Our love for fellow Christians, in other words, must have its roots in our love for God. John puts it unforgettably: "If any one says, 'I love God,' and hates his brother, he is a liar; for he who does not love his brother whom he has seen, cannot love God whom he has not seen" (I John 4:20).

But the other thought implied in the word "as" is that we are to accept one another *in the same manner* in which Christ has accepted us. How has Christ accepted us? In spite of our unworthiness—"God shows his love for us in that while we were yet sinners Christ died for us" (Rom. 5:8). Again, how has Christ accepted us? Without any partiality or discrimination. It makes not a particle of difference to Christ whether we are black or white, man or woman, young or old, Gentile or Jew, American or British, rich or poor, well educated or poorly educated. Now, says Paul, we are to accept one another as Christ has accepted us: not on the basis of merit, not because we like one man better than another, not on the basis of externals like money, nationality, or race—but simply because we are all in Christ together. I need no other reason for accepting you into full fellowship with me than that you are in Christ.

This point is so important that we should stop to think about it a little longer. If all this is true, we must realize that whenever we try to root our brotherhood with fellow Christians in something other than our oneness in Christ— say, in nationality, language, race, or ethnic background— we are acting in a basically unchristian manner. Dietrich Bonhoeffer, in his *Life Together,* makes a penetrating comment about this:

One who wants more than what Christ has established does not want Christian brotherhood. He is looking for some extraordinary social experience which he has not found elsewhere; he is bringing muddled and impure desires into Christian brotherhood. (p. 26)

Are our Christian communities entirely free from the tendency Bonhoeffer warns us against? In many evangelical congregations people who are not of the same ethnic or national background as the majority of the members find it very difficult to be totally accepted. That there is a good deal of clannishness and cliquishness in evangelical churches in America, for example, has been vividly demonstrated in a recent book by Marion Leach Jacobsen, *Saints and Snobs*. If I may speak of my own religious community, how hard it often is for a non-Dutchman to be accepted fully in a congregation whose members are mostly of Dutch descent! The same could be said, I am sure, of churches whose members are mostly of Swedish, Scottish, French, or German stock—to say nothing about the question of racial discrimination. The fact is that, to a larger extent than we realize or would like to admit, many of us who claim to be good Christians still do find our basis for unity even in the church in something other than our oneness in Christ. To the degree to which we do so, we fall short of the biblical ideal for the church.

Getting back now to Romans 15:7, it is to be noted that according to this passage we must accept each other as fellow members of the body of Christ despite our many differences. In the context of this text (that is, in chapters 14 and 15), Paul refers to two types of differences between Christians. One is the difference *between Jews and Gentiles*. It will be remembered that in Romans 11:18 Paul

had told the Gentile Christians that they should not look
down with disdain on Jewish Christians: "Do not boast
over the branches. If you do boast, remember it is not you
that support the root, but the root that supports you." He
is equally concerned that Jewish Christians should not look
down on Gentile Christians. Is the difference, now, between
black people and white people greater than that between
Jews and Gentiles? Let not the white Christian, then, look
down on the black Christian, and let not the black Christian look down on the white Christian. Let not the Occi-
dental Christian despise the Christian from the Orient. Let
not the Western Christian look with disdain upon the
Christian from the Third World.

The other type of difference referred to in the context
of Romans 15:7 is the difference *between strong Christians
and weak Christians.* Some of the Christians at Rome
thought it terribly wrong to eat meat which had been
offered to idols; others saw no wrong in this practice. Some
observed certain days in a special way (perhaps the old
Jewish feast days), whereas others considered all days
alike. Some apparently objected to drinking wine, while
others saw no harm in this. Paul urged them all not to sit
in judgment on each other. The questions involved in
these differences were not matters of principle, Paul ex-
plained, though some may have thought so. Because these
things were not matters of right and wrong, Paul urged
both the "strong" (those who saw no wrong in eating
meat offered to idols, drinking wine, and the like) and the
"weak" (those who had conscientious scruples about these
matters) to accept each other and to respect each other's
opinions.

Parallel to the situation in the Roman church to which

Paul was writing, there are today differences among Christians on such matters as the legitimacy of moderate smoking and drinking, and the use of cosmetics. Other items of this kind, which vary from culture to culture, could easily be mentioned. About such things, which are not matters of principle, the Scriptural rule is, "Accept one another as Christ accepted us." Paul even puts it as strongly as this: "Who are you to pass judgment on the servant of another? It is before his own master that he stands or falls" (Rom. 14:4).

The apostle tells us to accept one another as Christ has accepted us "to the glory of God." These words imply that when we do practice this acceptance, we glorify God. Glorifying God is not just a matter of singing lustily in church or putting a generous offering in the collection plate or teaching and defending sound doctrine, important as these things may be. Glorifying God includes such down-to-earth matters as welcoming strangers and accepting fellow Christians, not on the basis of race, nationality, or dress, but solely because they are in Christ. Conversely, our refusal to accept into our Christian fellowship people whom Christ has already accepted not only fails to glorify God; it is a sign of arrogant presumption.

How about our relation to non-Christians? In the passage we have been examining, Romans 15:7, Paul is specifically talking about the way we are to relate to fellow Christians. Our discussion so far in this chapter, therefore, has dealt only with the question of our accepting fellow Christians. Obviously, however, we must also have an attitude of acceptance toward non-Christians, including those of whom we are not sure whether they are Christians. The Bible teaches us that we owe love to every man, and love certainly includes acceptance. In this Christ Himself set us an example: He received "tax collectors and sinners," and even ate with them, to the consternation of the Pharisees. We must therefore have an attitude of acceptance toward every man, whether he be a Christian or not, regardless of his race, nationality, economic status, or social position. Needless to say, an attitude of acceptance toward non-Christians includes a genuine desire to lead them to Christ.

It should also be observed that an atmosphere of total acceptance within the church is of the utmost importance for the church's outreach into the world. If people who are not Christians see walls of prejudice, cliquishness, and snobbishness within a certain congregation, they will certainly not be inclined to join such a church, no matter how sound or active or famous it may be. Genuine love and mutual acceptance of one another within the church is an indispensable prerequisite for an effective evangelistic outreach. People are bound to be attracted by a fellowship of Christians which is genuinely open, joyful, and warm.

CHAPTER NINE

In Christ Together

Being in Christ has social dimensions. We are in Christ together, all of us who are Christians. In the last chapter one aspect of this togetherness was discussed—that of mutual acceptance. Let us now explore some further implications of our being in Christ together.

It would be an interesting experience for anyone to read through the entire New Testament to learn what kind of relationship with fellow Christians is there set before us, by example as well as by precept. When one does this, he will be amazed to see how far short we commonly fall of the Scriptural pattern for our life together. As we reflect on passages of this sort, we note five specific ways in which our oneness in Christ with fellow Christians is to express itself.

(1) Being in Christ together means, first of all, that *we must deal with each other as forgiven sinners*. What binds us together in Christ is not just that we are sinners but that we are forgiven sinners, justified sinners. This being the case, let us not be too harsh in our judgments of one another, but leave the final judgment up to God (I Cor. 4:5).

We must therefore always be ready to forgive one another, as God for Christ's sake has forgiven us (Eph. 4:32). To cherish a grudge against a fellow Christian or to continue to be bitter against him is contrary to Christ's command (Matt. 5:23-24; cf. Eph. 4:26).

The fact that we belong to a fellowship of forgiven sinners also implies that we must be willing, when necessary, to confess our sins to one another. James enjoins us, "Confess your sins to one another, and pray for one another, that you may be healed" (5:16). Dietrich Bonhoeffer stresses the importance of mutual confession of sin in the last chapter of his *Life Together*. He points out that many Christians, despite their being engaged in common prayer, common worship, and common service with fellow believers, remain ultimately lonely because they conceal their sins from one another. "The pious fellowship [Bonhoeffer's name for the kind of Christian group whose members are not open with each other] permits no one to be a sinner. So everybody must conceal his sin from himself and from the fellowship. We dare not be sinners" (p. 110). But when we have genuine fellowship in Christ, we dare to come to one another as fellow sinners, confessing our sins not only to God but also to our brothers and sisters. What inexpressible spiritual strengthening and comfort we receive when we do so! Quoting Bonhoeffer once again:

> In the presence of a psychiatrist I can only be a sick man; in the presence of a Christian brother I can dare to be a sinner. . . . The psychiatrist [obviously Bonhoeffer did not have a Christian psychiatrist in mind] views me as if there were no God. The brother views me as I am before the judging and merciful God in the Cross of Jesus Christ. (p. 119)

If it should some time be our unpleasant task to correct a brother who has fallen into sin, we must do so in the spirit of Galatians 6:1: "Brethren, if a man is overtaken in any trespass, you who are spiritual should restore him in a spirit of gentleness. Look to yourself, lest you too be tempted." What a difference it would make in our life together if all correction in the church were done in that spirit!

(2) Being in Christ together means, further, that *we should pray for one another.* Here Paul sets us an inspiring example. To the Colossians he writes, "And so . . . we have not ceased to pray for you, asking that you may be filled with the knowledge of his will in all spiritual wisdom and understanding, to lead a life worthy of the Lord, fully pleasing to him, bearing fruit in every good work and increasing in the knowledge of God" (1:9-10). To his spiritual son Timothy he writes, "I thank God whom I serve with a clear conscience, as did my fathers, when I remember you constantly in my prayers" (II Tim. 1:3). Is perhaps our life together often so far below par because we fail to pray for each other? James says, it will be recalled, "You do not have, because you do not ask" (4:2).

(3) Being in Christ together also means that *we should daily thank God for each other.* It is amazing to see how often Paul thanks God for people. Virtually every one of his letters begins with thanksgiving for what his fellow Christians mean to him: "I thank my God through Jesus Christ for all of you" (Rom. 1:8); "I thank my God in all my remembrance of you, always in every prayer of mine for you all making my prayer with joy" (Phil. 1:3-4); "But we are bound to give thanks to God always for you, brethren beloved by the Lord . . ." (II Thess. 2:13). Though, as

someone has said, the Corinthians gave Paul more head-
aches and heartaches than any other congregation, Paul gives
thanks also for them: "I give thanks to God always for
you because of the grace of God which was given you in
Christ Jesus" (I Cor. 1:4). Surely, fellowship with Christian
friends is one of life's greatest blessings, a constant source
of enrichment, encouragement, and joy! Surely, too, our
common failure to thank God daily for our Christian friends
is one of the most telling evidences of our ingratitude.

(4) Being in Christ together means that *we must see
Christ in each other.* To be in Christ, as we have seen,
means to be in Christ with others. Paul says in Romans
12:4 and 5, "For as in one body we have many members,
and all the members do not have the same function, so we,
though many, are one body in Christ, and individually members one of another." The figure of the body and its members tells us that we must not just see Christ in ourselves;
we must also see Christ in our Christian brothers. When I
look at you, my Christian brother, my first impulse should
not be to see what fault I can find with you; it should
be to see what Christ has done for you and is doing through
you. I must thank God for the enrichment He gives me
through you, and I must listen for what Christ is trying to
tell me through you. Here lies the difference between the
Christian and the atheistic existentialist. For the existentialist, other people get in the way of our freedom and thus
become our torturers. In his play *No Exit,* Jean-Paul Sartre
says, "Hell is other people." But the Christian says, "I thank
God for people, for through people in whom Christ lives
God is constantly enriching my life."

Seeing Christ in one another implies that we rejoice in
one another and in what God is doing through the other

person. Whatever it is in us that delights in gossiping about our brother's sins, it is not of the Holy Spirit. Paul again gives us a good example here: he rejoiced at the good things that were happening to his Christian friends. To the Colossians he wrote, "Though I am absent in body, yet I am with you in spirit, rejoicing to see your good order and the firmness of your faith in Christ" (2:5). After having expressed gratitude for the reports conveyed to him about the faith and love of the Thessalonians, Paul went on to say, "For what thanksgiving can we render to God for you, for all the joy which we feel for your sake before our God . . . ?" (I Thess. 3:9). The Apostle John expressed a similar sentiment in his third epistle, the fourth verse: "No greater joy can I have than this, to hear that my children follow the truth."

Another implication of seeing Christ in each other is that we have confidence in one another. We tend to mistrust each other. Paul did not share this kind of mistrust of his Christian brothers. To the Thessalonians he wrote, "And we have confidence in the Lord about you, that you are doing and will do the things which we command" (II Thess. 3:4). And to Philemon, whom he asks to take back his runaway slave as a Christian brother, he writes, "Confident of your obedience, I write to you, knowing that you will do even more than I say" (v. 21). We may conclude that the Lord wants each of us to have this kind of confidence in one another.

Still another implication of our seeing Christ in each other is a readiness to encourage each other. Sometimes it may be necessary for me to rebuke my Christian brother or sister, but that person may need my word of encouragement today as much as he or she will need my word of rebuke tomorrow. Note again what Paul says to the Thessalonians: "For you know how, like a father with his children, we exhorted each one of you and encouraged you . . ." (I Thess. 2:11). He makes a point, in fact, of telling the Thessalonians that this is what they should also be doing for one another: "Therefore encourage one another and build one another up, just as you are doing" (I Thess. 5:11).

(5) Finally, being in Christ together means that *we must maintain our unity in Christ*. Some Christians seem more eager to divide believers than to keep them together. But consider how Paul pleaded with the Corinthians to maintain their unity: "I appeal to you, brethren, by the name of our Lord Jesus Christ, that all of you agree and that there be no dissensions among you, but that you be united in the same mind and the same judgment" (I Cor. 1:10). Note his appeal to the Ephesians: "I therefore, a prisoner for the Lord, beg you to lead a life worthy of the calling to which you have been called . . . eager to maintain the unity of the Spirit in the bond of peace" (4:1, 3). That Paul felt very deeply about this matter is evident from his words to the Philippians: "So if there is any encouragement in Christ, any incentive of love, any participation in the Spirit, any affection and sympathy, complete my joy by being of the same mind, having the same love, being in full accord and of one mind" (2:1-2).

Surely we must take these passages to heart. At a time when internal dissensions threaten to divide many Christians from each other, and to split not only congregations but denominations, how urgently we need to remember that if we are truly in Christ the points on which we differ are always less important than the basic verities on which we agree. When we who claim to be in Christ together cannot live in unity with one another, what kind of witness are we giving to the world? Let the words of Christ's high-priestly prayer continue to ring in our ears: "I do not pray for these only, but also for those who believe in me through their word, that they may all be one; even as thou, Father, art in me, and I in thee, that they also may be in us, so that the world may believe that thou hast sent me" (John 17:20-21).

PART II: IMPLEMENTATION

CHAPTER TEN

What Can I Do About It?

We have tried in Part I to see what the Scriptures teach us about the way we who claim to be Christians ought to look at ourselves and at our fellow Christians. But now the question remains, How can we make these insights part of our daily experience? How can we translate them from the theological realm into the psychological? How can we move them from the nebulous area of theoretical abstraction into the arena of daily life?

Here, for example, is a man who says: I know and accept all these doctrines you have been expounding. I believe what the Bible teaches about the new man, the new creature, the indwelling of the Holy Spirit, and the like. But I still have my problems. I still have a negative self-image. I can accept all these doctrines with my head, but they do not make me stop despising myself.

I feel extremely unworthy, the man goes on to say. I try to fight against my sins, but it seems to do very little good. I not only keep on sinning, I keep falling into the same sins. Though my faults have been pointed out to me many times, I still have them. According to the Bible I'm supposed to be a new creature—but I don't see much newness in me. Instead, I see a lot of the old. The old self or the old nature is always cropping up. So how can I have a positive self-image?

Let me say first of all that the problems of the person who talks this way may lie, and usually do lie, at a much deeper level than the intellectual. Merely reasoning with such a person will probably not help him much. The roots of his troubles probably lie in childhood experiences which have left an indelible mark on his personality, or in certain religious presuppositions which have been drilled into him and which he cannot shake off. There are types of churches in which the primary emphasis of the pulpit is on sin and misery, and in which the message of forgiving grace is all but eclipsed. In these churches only a handful of people partake of the Lord's Supper, since most members do not have enough assurance of their salvation to feel that they can take communion without "eating and drinking damnation to themselves." If a person has been brought up in a church of this sort, he will have an extremely difficult time maintaining a positive self-image.

What can be done for such a person? This is difficult to say. It might well be that a person of this sort ought to submit to a program of intensive psychological therapy at the hands of a competent counselor. Or perhaps a pastor with some training in counseling could help. It is also possible that a person with problems as deep-seated as these will never be able to attain a consistently positive self-image.

In a book like this we can only advance certain rational considerations. These, as was already suggested, will have a limited value. But they might be appealed to by a skillful counselor in such a way as to be eventually helpful.

By way of replying, then, to the person whose problem was described above, let me advance the following observations. These considerations will not be totally new, but will be elaborations of points already made.

(1) The reader is reminded of what was said in Chapter 7 about the impossibility of attaining sinless perfection in this present life, and about the tension between the already and the not-yet in which we continually live. If, as Paul says in Romans 8:23, we have only the first fruits of the Spirit, we should not expect to attain total perfection on this side of the grave. If even James had to say, "For in many things we all stumble" (3:2, ASV), we should not be surprised that we also still stumble.

It is extremely important that we retain this realistic understanding of ourselves, lest we become unduly discouraged. And yet, as we noted, the fact that we cannot reach perfection in this life does not imply that our self-image must be predominantly negative. For though the New Testament teaches that we do continue to sin after we become believers, it lays its emphasis not on our continuing sinfulness, but on our newness in Christ.

(2) The reader is further reminded that although the believer has decisively put off the "old man" and put on the "new man" (see Chapter 3), this does not mean that we never slip back into an "old-man" way of living. We all know that we do—not just occasionally, but frequently. In a sense, therefore, it is true that the struggle of life for the believer is that between the new life-style and the old, and that as long as we are in this life, the new never completely replaces the old.

But this does not imply that we must make the old

man an integral part of our self-image. As we have seen, Scripture teaches that we are now new men in Christ, and that insofar as we still do slip into old-man ways of living, we are living contrary to our true selves.

Right at this point, however, I can imagine a person such as the one we have described saying something like this: "But all this doesn't help me one bit. You're just playing a word-game with me. I don't really care what names you give to one thing or another. I don't really care whether you say that I'm living up to my true self or my false self. The fact remains that I'm constantly slipping into old-man ways of living. And how can I then still maintain a positive image of myself?"

Let us once again look at this question in the light of New Testament teachings. If the old man is considered an inescapable part of me, I then have a handy, built-in excuse for sinning. Whenever I do something wrong, I can always say, "Oh, but I can't help doing that; you see, that's the old man in me." But this kind of reasoning is precisely what the Bible warns us against. The old man is the old self which I repudiated when I became a Christian. It is no longer part of me. I am now a new person in Christ, who has voluntarily adopted a new life-style. When I therefore slip back into an old-man way of living, I have no excuse. All I can do is to confess that I did wrong, and to try again in the strength of the Spirit to live in accordance with my real self. Holding on to the positive self-image the Bible prescribes, therefore, should be a deterrent to slipping back into wrong ways of living.

But, one might ask, how can we hold on to this positive self-image? The positive self-image the Bible teaches us to have is an item of faith, to be accepted like every other item of faith. Continuing to cling to this image, therefore, is a matter of continuing to believe that what the Bible says about us is true. What the Bible says about us who are in Christ is that we are now new creatures.

Faith in the fact of our newness is an essential aspect of the Christian life. As John says, "This is the victory that overcomes the world, our faith" (I John 5:4). Apart from this faith, we are doomed to defeat. Failing to accept our newness in Christ is to believe the devil's lie instead of God's truth.

But, one might still ask, should not this newness be so evident and visible in our lives that we do not need to have faith to accept it? There is a sense in which this is true, since even Jesus said, "By their fruits ye shall know them" (Matt. 7:20, ASV). But there remains a sense in which this newness is always an object of faith. There is something hidden about the Christian's new life: "your life is hid with Christ in God," Paul said to the Colossians (3:3). Since we live in eschatological tension between the already and the not-yet, we do not yet see this newness in its totality. We must therefore continue to accept it by faith.

One more thing should be said in connection with the distinction between the old man and the new. As was also mentioned in Chapter 7, the new man which believers have put on is being continually renewed. We there noted Paul's words in Colossians 3:9-10: "Lie not one to another; seeing that ye have put off the old man with his doings, and have put on the new man, that is being renewed unto knowledge after the image of him that created him" (ASV).

This fact has some important implications. A rather

common view of the new man is that it means sinless perfection. According to this view, the old-man part of me still sins, but the new-man part of me is sinless. A Christian holding to this view will, of course, not dare to think of himself as a new man, since, if he is honest with himself, he will know that he does not live without sin. But the concept of the new man found in Colossians 3:10 is a much more realistic one. According to this passage the new man which we have put on needs to be continually renewed (the verb form used here is in the present tense, implying continuing action). The new man described in this passage, therefore, cannot mean sinless perfection—for if it did, why should it need to be continually renewed? When I think of the new man in this way, I can think of myself as a new man without claiming to live in sinless perfection.

The fact that we must be continually transformed (which is taught, for example, in Rom. 12:2 and II Cor. 3:18) implies that we can afford to be realistic about ourselves. We could perhaps put it this way: we are *genuinely* new, but not yet *totally* new. Total newness will come by and by. But already now it is true that I have put off the old self, that old self which was crucified with Christ. I must therefore continue to see myself as a new person in Christ, who needs to be continually renewed.

(3) A third observation ties in with what was developed in Chapter 5 in connection with the problem of spiritual pride: the Christian self-image is ultimately based, not on our own achievements, but on God's gracious acceptance of us in Christ. We are new creatures, *not apart from Christ, but only in Christ.* Our positive self-image, therefore, is not rooted in human merit but in divine grace.

This observation should keep a person from denying that he can have a positive self-image in the Christian sense because he continues to be a sinner. One who would base his positive self-image primarily on his own accomplishments would be guilty of Pharisaism.

There is, however, another side to this question. Though the Christian self-image is rooted in divine grace, one cannot expect to continue to enjoy a positive self-image if he is living irresponsibly. Every Christian should see himself as a new creature in Christ. But this newness must reveal itself at least to some extent in a new way of living— responsible living, if you will. Paul put it well when he said that Christ died for us "that those who live might live no longer for themselves but for him who for their sake died and was raised" (II Cor. 5:15). Elsewhere Paul, writing to mature believers, says, "I urge you, brothers, in view of God's mercy, to offer yourselves as living sacrifices, holy and pleasing to God—which is your spiritual worship" (Rom. 12:1, NIV). And in one place he even uses the word "worthy" to describe this kind of living: "I therefore, a prisoner for the Lord, beg you to lead a life worthy of the calling to which you have been called" (Eph. 4:1).

The point is not, of course, that believers can perfectly reveal this newness during the present life. But it remains true that the Christian faith cannot be exercised in a vacuum. The faith which we have in Christ is a faith which works through love (Gal. 5:6). James reminds us that faith without works is dead (James 2:26). Though our positive self-image must ultimately be rooted in what Christ has done for us, our lives must continue to reflect the evidence of Christ's presence in us.

One writer who has done some reflecting on this theme

is William Glasser. He believes that responsible behavior is basic to the maintenance of a positive self-image. The following quotation summarizes his position:

> . . . *To be worthwhile we must maintain a satisfactory standard of behavior.* . . . If we do not evaluate our own behavior, or having evaluated it, we do not act to improve our conduct where it is below our standards, we will not fulfill our need to be worthwhile and we will suffer as acutely as when we fail to love or be loved. Morals, standards, values, or right and wrong behavior are all intimately related to the fulfillment of our need for self-worth. . . . (*Reality Therapy,* pp. 10-11)

Glasser's statement must, of course, not be understood apart from what was said earlier about the rooting of our self-image in God's gracious acceptance of us. Yet even the Bible teaches that the new self which we have put on must reveal itself in new ways of living: "Do not lie to each other, since you have taken off your old self with its practices and have put on the new self, which is being renewed in knowledge in the image of its Creator" (Col. 3:9-10, NIV).

If, then, we have not been living responsibly as Christians, this must be rectified if we wish to enjoy a positive Christian self-image. We may have been living only for ourselves, quite unconcerned about the needs, problems, and sufferings of our fellowmen. We may have been living primarily for personal enjoyment, material things, social advancement, or professional prestige. We may have been manipulating people for our own purposes instead of loving them and helping them. We may have been playing God, with self on the throne, while God and others occupy subordinate places. Instead of surrendering our lives to God for the doing of His will, we may have been using Him to advance our own purposes.

One cannot continue to enjoy the benefits of the Christian self-image while living either deliberately or half-consciously contrary to God's will. If a person who complains that he cannot maintain a positive Christian self-image should be one whose life answers to the above description, there is only one solution to his problem: total surrender to God. Such surrender does not mean the attainment of sinless perfection, but the genuine desire and deliberate choice to live, not for self, but for God and His kingdom. It means that the basic direction of one's life is toward God and not toward himself.

There must therefore be a kind of balance in our lives. We must rest on the grace of God for our full acceptance as His children. At the same time we must reveal the genuineness of our faith by lives which have been surrendered to God. Without such surrender we shall not be able to maintain a positive Christian self-image.

CHAPTER ELEVEN

What Can Others Do About It?

In the previous chapter we saw what a person who accepts the Christian message but is still troubled by a negative self-image can do about solving his problem. In this chapter we shall go on to ask what others can do to help a person attain and maintain the kind of positive self-image which is an essential aspect of the Christian faith.

We shall be looking at the role of the pastor, the counselor, the teacher, and the parent. What can each of these do to help people attain the kind of self-image we have been discussing?

The ultimate basis for our positive self-image must be God's acceptance of us in Christ. Though this is true, it is equally true that this divine acceptance is communicated to us through people. One of the most important ways in which others can help us maintain a positive self-image is to communicate to us the fact that God has fully accepted us in Christ.

Our image of ourselves is also based in part on whether our fellowmen accept us or reject us. One will not be likely to maintain a positive self-image if he feels totally rejected by his peers. A second significant role, therefore, which pastors, counselors, teachers, and parents can play is to reveal, both verbally and nonverbally, their total acceptance of the persons to whom they minister. Such total acceptance, needless to say, involves love. The biblical injunction, "Owe no one anything, except to love one another" (Rom. 13:8), is certainly applicable to persons in the helping professions and to parents.

We go on now to ask what various things pastors, counselors, teachers, and parents can do to help others maintain a biblical self-image.

The most important thing a *pastor* can do, it seems to me, is to *give his people a balanced presentation of the total message of the Bible.* Earlier in the book we noted that preachers may convey distorted understandings of the Bible which can easily lead their hearers to have negative images of themselves. We looked at some concrete examples of this (see above, pp. 16, 18, 94).

Another example may be helpful. This one is taken from the life of John Bunyan, the author of *Pilgrim's Progress.* In his autobiography, *Grace Abounding to the Chief of Sinners,* he tells how on many mornings he was cast into the depths of depression by the crushing impact of certain terrifying Bible texts which he could not shrug off. One such text was the passage in Hebrews 12 which speaks of Esau's finding "no chance to repent, though he sought it with tears" (v. 17). I knew, Bunyan tells us, that this text described me, for had I not also sold my spiritual birthright when I said that I was willing to renounce Christ? Had I not therefore committed the unpardonable sin? So it would go with me, Bunyan continues, until later in the day, when some "happy text" promising pardon and peace to all who truly repent would spring into my mind. Then my soul would leap with joy unspeakable, and I would be happy again.

It was not until Bunyan had learned to grasp the total message of the Bible, particularly its message of full and free forgiveness for penitent sinners, that he found the peace of soul he had been looking for. His experiences remind us of the importance of preaching the full counsel of God, the total gospel of redemption, to people who may be troubled by similar doubts.

The preacher must bring to his people a balanced presentation of the gospel. He must preach not only about sin but also about redemption, not only about guilt but also about the removal of guilt. And the emphasis of his preaching should fall where it falls in the Bible: not on the sin but on the grace, not on condemnation but on salvation. What stands out in the New Testament, like a rainbow coming out of a cloud, is the triumphant message of redemption and renewal: the believer is now a new creature in Christ! And this is where the preacher's emphasis should fall. To lay the stress on the continued sinfulness of the believer rather than on his newness in Christ is to turn the New Testament upside down!

Let the preacher, therefore, unfold for his people the tremendous resources of the Christian faith for a positive self-image. What these resources are we have already seen. Let him preach often about the exhilaration of forgiveness, about the joy of knowing that our sins are totally pardoned, buried in the sea of God's forgetfulness. Let him preach about the believer as a new person, as a new creature in Christ, as one who is indwelt by the Holy Spirit, as one who is being progressively transformed into the image of Christ. Let him remind his hearers that Christianity does not only mean believing something about Jesus Christ, but that it also means believing something about ourselves. For a proper Christian self-image is an essential aspect of our Christian faith. Let the preacher not allow the atheist or the agnostic to tell him what kind of self-image the Christian ought to have; let the preacher speak from his own faith in God's promises and from his own experience of God's mercies.

Let us consider next what a *counselor* can do to help his clients attain the kind of self-image the Bible wants them to have. We shall think specifically of the Christian counselor, and assume that he is dealing with Christian people and can therefore appeal to biblical teachings in his counseling procedures.

The primary goal of the Christian counselor, it seems to me, ought to be to *help his client apply to his or her own life what the Bible teaches about the Christian self-image.* Let the counselor try to remove whatever may be hindering the client from accepting these biblical teachings. Perhaps what the client needs most is to be assured that he is indeed a worthy person in God's sight—a person who is not only a creature of God but also an object of God's redemptive love. Perhaps the client needs to be reassured that there is a sense in which he may and indeed should love himself in order that he may properly love his fellowman. Certainly he needs to see the love of God for him reflected through the counselor's own warm acceptance of him as a person.

What, now, are some specific procedures a counselor might use to help his client attain this goal? One such procedure might be *significant dialogue, in which the client is helped to evaluate himself realistically*. Such dialogue could serve to call the client's attention to his or her strong points and to suggest ways in which these strong points could be put to better use. The ensuing discussion could reveal that the client has been making too much of his failures and placing too low a value on his competencies. In this way the counselor could help the client arrive at a more realistic and balanced evaluation of himself.

In this connection the counselor could call the client's attention to Romans 12:3: "For by the grace given to me I bid every one among you not to think of himself more highly than he ought to think, but to think with sober judgment, each according to the measure of faith which God has assigned him." Though this passage warns us against thinking of ourselves more highly than we ought to think, by implication it also warns us against thinking of ourselves less highly than we ought to think. Thinking "with sober judgment," it seems to me, means accepting ourselves as God made us, and not trying to be someone other than we are. Such acceptance implies recognizing whatever abilities we do have as given by God and using them in His service.

Another procedure a counselor might use is to *explore the possibilities of group counseling*. One therapist found it most helpful to conduct a class on Sunday mornings for a period of three months at a time. He calls this class an "adult elective," and entitles it "Christian Mental Health and its Applications." As he puts it, "Our goal is to increase our understanding of ourselves and our family relationships, in order to (1) promote self-acceptance and (2) make it easier for God to love others through us"

(Kirk E. Farnsworth, "Love Your Neighbor as Much as You Love Yourself," in *Proceedings of the Christian Association for Psychological Studies*, 1971, pp. 60-61).

It might be profitable to note some of the things Farnsworth says about the way he conducts this class:

> In order to improve my regard for myself, and thereby improve my relations with my neighbor, I need to be confronted with my strong points in a meaningful way and receive honest, immediate feedback as I react to others. Threfore, it is crucial that the adult elective be as interaction- and experience-centered as possible. Although only minimally confrontive, the group openly shares and is supportive. We pray for and with each other, by name and with real expectancy, sharing the results of our daily involvement each Sunday morning. Also during the week, we carry out "experiments in faith" to help us put into practice what we discuss each Sunday.
>
> . . . In order to develop the idea and the experience of self-esteem, four broad areas are usually presented, in outline form, for class discussion: (a) Self-Discovery; (b) Self-Expression; (c) Self-Deception; (d) Self-Acceptance. The goal is to *see* me (self-discovery), to *free* me (self-expression), and to *be* me (self-acceptance). A wide variety of topics are discussed within each area, culminating in the final area—Self-Acceptance—with a look at self-love. (p. 61)

Another way in which a counselor might bring the benefits of group reaction to bear on an individual would be to ask him to take part in group-therapy sessions. In sessions of this sort, usually limited to not more than ten people, participants are encouraged to be completely open with each other, and to discuss freely one another's negative and positive traits, with the emphasis on the positive. Because of the delicacy of the relationships involved and the danger that things might get out of hand and lead to negative results, it is extremely important that the leader of such a group be a competent person, well trained in the psychological and interpersonal procedures involved.

Ideally, of course, this group therapy is practiced among fellow Christians, who are able to strengthen each other in the faith and help each other appropriate the resources of that faith for the deepening of their fellowship. If, as we all recognize, the love of God for us is channeled through other people, what a marvelously enriching experience it is to see that others love us and accept us! When group therapy as described above is skillfully conducted, those involved will be confirmed in their conviction that they are fully accepted by God and by their fellow Christians, and that they should therefore also fully accept themselves.

Still another way in which a counselor could help his client arrive at a more positive self-image would be to *try to help him achieve some kind of success.* Many writers in this field have pointed out that in order to have a positive self-image a person must feel that he has succeeded at something in his life. It does not matter a great deal whether the success achieved is in an area highly esteemed by educated people or even by the general public; what matters is that it be in an area which is significant for the individual concerned. The solving of a complicated accounting problem, for example, can be as important an achievement for one person as the writing of a symphony might be for another.

Abraham Maslow has some interesting things to say about this. In his *Toward a Psychology of Being* he tells us that he had mistakenly been thinking of creativeness only in connection with certain areas of human endeavor like painting, music, and poetry:

But these expectations were broken up by various of my subjects. For instance, one woman, uneducated, poor, a full-time housewife and mother, did none of these conventionally creative things and yet was a marvellous cook, mother, wife and homemaker. With little money, her home was somehow always beautiful. She was a perfect hostess. Her meals were banquets. Her taste in linens, silver, glass, crockery and furniture was impeccable. She was in all these areas original, novel, ingenious, unexpected, inventive. I just *had* to call her creative. I learned from her and others like her that a first-rate soup is more creative than a second-rate painting, and that, generally, cooking or parenthood or making a home could be creative while poetry need not be; it could be uncreative. (p. 136)

In this connection the counselor could point out that according to Scriptural teaching everyone has gifts and everyone is expected to use his gifts in God's service. The point of the Parable of the Talents in Matthew 25 is not the superior value of the person who had five talents over him who had only two, but the faithfulness with which each servant worked with the talents he had. And the figure of the body with many members in I Corinthians 12 underscores the fact that every member of Christ's body serves an important function: "The eye cannot say to the hand, 'I have no need of you,' nor again the head to the feet, 'I have no need of you'" (v. 21). In the faithful use of whatever gifts and abilities we have, therefore, every one of us is to find his own achievements and successes.

A final suggestion for counselors is this: *Try to get the client to overcome irresponsible behavior.* In the previous chapter it was emphasized that responsible Christian living is essential to maintaining a positive self-image. If a client has not lived responsibly, the counselor may be able to help him or her to rectify matters.

The counselor, then, must not feel that accepting the client necessarily implies approving of everything he does. As a matter of fact, calling the counselee's attention to irresponsible behavior is evidence, not of hatred, but of love— as long as the counselor makes clear that while rejecting his client's wrong behavior he still accepts his person. Not only should the counselor reject the client's irresponsible behavior; he should also help the counselee find more responsible ways of fulfilling his needs. Preferably the counselor does this indirectly, leading the client himself to map out a new course of action.

We go on now to ask what the *teacher* can do to help his or her pupils gain a more positive image of themselves. Though what will be said here applies to all teachers, we shall be thinking particularly about teachers in the elementary grades, since the first years of school are of basic significance for the formation of a child's self-image. It will be assumed that the teacher we are talking about is a Christian, whether he or she be teaching in a public school or in a Christian school.

It is most important, first of all, that the Christian teacher *help each pupil understand that God loves him.* This may be done by either direct or indirect means. In a school where the Christian teacher is not free to give full expression to her Christian convictions, she will do her best to communicate God's love for every child by her own attitude toward her pupils and her own way of dealing with them. By expressing her love for the children under her care, she can help each child feel that he or she is of value.

If, on the other hand, the teacher is teaching in a Christian school, where she has complete freedom to express her

Christian beliefs, she will be able to communicate God's love for the children more directly. She will be able to tell her pupils that God loves and cares for each child as His creature, and that He has showered His blessings on each one of them. She can go on to say, in the words of John 3:16, "God so loved the world that he gave his only Son, that whoever believes in him should not perish but have eternal life." The teacher can then explain that the blessing of salvation from sin is conditional upon faith, repentance, and commitment to Christ. Not only children whose parents are not Christians but also children born of Christian parents must personally repent and believe. Membership in the covenant of grace (which is the privilege of children from Christian homes) does not exclude but includes the need for total commitment to Christ. The teacher should make clear that it is only after such a commitment has been made that a person can fully enjoy the benefits of a Christian self-image.

Furthermore, the teacher should do her best to *help each child feel that he is accepted by others*. This means first of all total acceptance by the teacher. How can the teacher demonstrate such total acceptance? He or she must approach each student with an attitude of warmth and of respect for the uniqueness of each child's personality. Specific ways in which a teacher can communicate acceptance include giving each pupil as much encouragement as possible, and stimulating growing independence in her pupils. Excessive dependence on the teacher goes hand in hand with low self-esteem. Children should be trained to make decisions for themselves already in their younger years, so that they will begin to feel significant.

Acceptance by others includes acceptance by the child's

classmates. What can the teacher do to improve this? One thing the teacher can do is to create a classroom atmosphere in which students accept and help each other. It is important that a child learns to make a realistic appraisal of his own abilities and limitations. But it is equally important that each child in a class learns to accept and appreciate his classmates, with their particular abilities and limitations—neither envying his more gifted classmates nor belittling the less gifted ones.

Let the teacher, then, find ways in which the brighter children in the class can help the slower ones. Let the teacher encourage the brighter children to cheer on the slower learners as they make progress, and to be happy along with them when they do well. Let the teacher also find ways in which the less gifted children can contribute significantly to the class, especially in areas where they are strong.

Another way in which the teacher can encourage pupils to accept each other is to get them involved in group projects. Both slow learners and rapid learners often feel that they are not fully accepted by their classmates—the latter because they are afraid that others are jealous of their gifts or higher marks. If students are directed to work in groups, so that those of varying abilities will have to work together, the class as a whole will better be able to appreciate the unique contributions each child can make.

We come now to the most crucial role of all—that of the Christian *parent*. It is in the home that a child's basic attitude toward himself is formed. The most important source of a child's self-image is the response he receives in the home, especially from his parents: the way they look at him, the way they talk about him, whether they accept or reject him.

It must, of course, be granted that homes differ a great deal from each other. Some homes are wealthy, while others are poor; some parents are well educated, whereas others have had little or no formal education. Matters like education or wealth, however, have little to do with the kind of image a child forms of himself. Contrary to popular opinion, self-esteem does not depend on physical appearance, wealth, or education, and is only slightly related to social status and academic performance. What is of primary importance is the way a person is treated by people significant to him, be they parents or peers. Loving acceptance by his parents will do more than anything else to give a child a positive self-image.

What, now, can Christian parents do to help their children have the kind of self-image the Scriptures hold before us? Once again it must be said that what is of primary importance is the child's relationship to God. Christian parents must therefore *communicate to their children the fact that they belong to God and are the heirs of the promises and blessings of God's covenant of grace.* This must be done both verbally and nonverbally. Long before a child can begin to understand words about God, parents must reveal God's love for the child through the love they show to him. Parents should show as much love to their children as they possibly can, remembering that a child's understanding of God is primarily a reflection of the way he views his parents, both his mother and his father.

As the child grows older, the parents should instruct him in the good news of the gospel—not only the promises of the covenant but also the responsibilities which covenant membership entails. For covenant children, as well as for those not born of Christian parents, salvation is conditional upon repentance and faith. Christian parents, therefore, should prayerfully try to lead each child, as he becomes old enough to do so, to commit himself and his life to Christ. Parents should then help the son or daughter understand that as a committed believer he or she is now indeed a new creature in Christ, and that having this kind of self-image is an essential aspect of the Christian faith.

Parents should also *communicate to their children the fact that they are totally accepted by father and mother.* This can be done in various ways. One of the most important ways is to tell their children that they love them. It is a serious mistake for parents to fail to express love for their children, believing that this is unnecessary: "Of course our children know that we love them!" The fact of the matter is that children often long to be reassured of their parents' love for them. This is particularly true when some kind of discipline has been administered. It should be made very clear to a child that disapproval of his actions does not mean rejection of his person.

Thomas Gordon, in his *Parent Effectiveness Training,* offers the example of a mother whose daughter had promised to be home from her date no later than midnight, but did not actually return home until 1:30. The mother, who had not been able to sleep while waiting for her daughter, greeted her at the door with the words, "I'm angry with you!" The instructor of the class in which this incident was reported asked the mother, "How did you really feel when Linda walked in?" The mother replied, "I felt terribly relieved that she was home safe. I wanted to hug her and tell her so." The instructor then said, "Why didn't you tell her so? Why didn't you say, 'Oh, Linda, thank God you're home safe. I'm so glad to see you'? Later you could decide on whatever disciplinary measures might still need to be administered. But at the moment it was important that your daughter should realize how much she meant to you" (pp. 123-24).

Another way in which parents can indicate that they accept their children is to show a genuine interest in them and in their activities. This includes concern for both successes and failures. If parents take a child's successes for granted but discipline or upbraid him for his failures, the child may easily get the impression that his parents do not fully accept him. Though parents should neither encourage nor approve deliberate underachievement in their children, they should be sympathetic and understanding when a child fails. And they should not be stingy with their praise when a child succeeds. Too little praise may be more damaging to a child than too much.

Still another way in which parents can communicate acceptance to their children is by being available in times of discomfort or distress. In this way parents can demonstrate that they accept their children not only when matters are running smoothly, but also when the children are in trouble. Parents should make themselves available not just when the problems of their children are of major proportions, but even when the difficulties might seem minor. Whether what makes a child run to mother is a skinned knee or a runover puppy, to a child no problem is unimportant.

In this connection a word may be said about what Thomas Gordon calls "active listening" (*Parent Effectiveness Training,* pp. 49-94). By "active listening" he means a

kind of listening in which one does his very best to understand what the other person is saying, and particularly to
understand what he is feeling. For example, when a child
storms into the house extremely angry because of something
one of his playmates has just done, the mother who is
listening actively will resist the temptation to scold the
child for losing his temper, and will say to him, "I see you're
terribly angry about something." The child will then usually
tell what it is he is angry about, and the mother will be
able to help him solve his problem more effectively than if
she had simply scolded him. A mother must let her child
know that she understands the child's feelings, and accepts
him as he is, with all his feelings.

A child should feel accepted not just by his parents and
teachers, but also by his peers. Another important way in
which parents can help their children develop positive
images of themselves, therefore, is to try to *create an atmosphere in the home in which the children accept each
other*. The children should be encouraged to appreciate
each other's talents and gifts, and to cheer each other along
when they learn new skills or make other kinds of progress.
Needless to say, parents should be extremely careful not to
show favoritism in the home. The Bible story about Jacob's
favoritism toward his son Joseph reminds us that it is not
always easy for parents to treat all their children impartially.
And yet a prayerful effort must be made to do so.

Parents should also *handle disciplinary problems in such
a way as not to damage a child's positive self-image*. A home
without discipline is a poor home; yet much depends on the
way in which discipline is handled. The most important
thing to remember, it seems to me, is that discipline in the

home must be an expression of love for the child and an affirmation, not a denial, of his worth.

Parents should set firm but reasonable restrictions for their children's behavior. On the basis of extensive research Stanley Coopersmith found that, contrary to the opinion of many, it is not the permissive homes that produce children with positive self-images, but the homes which maintain and enforce parental restrictions. His words on this point are worth quoting: ". . . Higher levels of self-esteem are associated with greater demands, firmer regulation, and parental decisiveness rather than with a tension-free, permissive, and otherwise idealized environment" (*The Antecedents of Self-Esteem*, p. 261).

That parents set restrictions for their children's behavior is, of course, to be expected in Christian homes, where it is believed that right and wrong behavior are not just determined by human tradition or social custom, but are the expression of the will of God. Yet two cautions should be kept in mind in connection with the setting of restrictions. First, restrictions and rules must be in the context of acceptance and love. The mere adoption of restrictions apart from total acceptance will not build a child's self-image, since if a child does not feel accepted he may well interpret parental restrictions as evidence of hostility and rejection. But if a child knows that his parents love him, he will, at least in his better moments, interpret restrictions and discipline as evidence of caring and concern.

The second caution is this: The rules and restrictions imposed by parents must not be unreasonable, harsh, arbitrary, or inflexible. The purpose of these rules is not to establish the superior power of the parent over the child, but to guide the child into ways of behavior which are acceptable to God and to other people. Parental rules, therefore, should define the bounds of what is permissible in such a way as not to destroy the child's belief in his or her own worth.

The question may be asked, How do parental restrictions help a child build a positive self-image? If the limits set by parents are reasonable, and if the child knows that his parents love and accept him, the child who has tried to comply with his parents' restrictions will have a clear and relatively unequivocal basis for judging himself and for evaluating his personal worth. Such a child has a set of values to judge himself by. In an extremely permissive home, however, where a child is allowed to do anything he pleases, and where there do not seem to be any parental norms for his behavior except that he should not bother his parents too much, a child will lack a clear set of values. A child brought up in such a home will find it difficult to judge himself either favorably or unfavorably, and will remain in a state of doubt about his personal worth (see Coopersmith, p. 208).

It needs to be added that Christian parents will point their children to the biblical message of forgiveness for sin when rules have been broken or restrictions have been transgressed. It is important that a child learns to see that disobedience to parents is disobedience to God (since God has given parents authority over their children), but it is just as important that he learns about the forgiving mercy of God.

Yet parents should be careful not to make all their rules for their children equivalent to the laws of God. Some things are matters of right and wrong, but other things are simply matters of taste or parental preference. Not all instances in which children do things of which their parents disapprove need to be punished. In fact, parents do not always need to make rules; sometimes it is better for them simply to express a preference for certain types of behavior.

Often it is possible to solve conflicts between parents and children over matters of behavior by means of what Thomas Gordon calls the "no-lose" method (*Parent Effectiveness Training,* chapter 11). Here a conflict is resolved by a joint search for a solution which will be acceptable to both parent and child. Gordon gives the following example: Daughter Jane was about to leave for school on a rainy morning without her raincoat. The reason, her father soon learned, was that her raincoat was plaid, and nobody at school would be wearing a plaid raincoat. The father, however, did not want Jane to catch a cold or ruin her clothes. So he said, "Can you think of a solution we both could accept?" Whereupon Jane replied, "Maybe I could borrow Mom's car coat today." After mother's permission had been obtained, Jane went off to school wearing the car coat, and both she and her father were satisfied with the solution they had arrived at together (pp. 196-97). In this method of resolving conflicts no punishment is required, no parental enforcement of rules is needed, and the conflict becomes the occasion for expressing love rather than hostility. Since the child himself or herself has played a significant part in finding the solution, his or her self-image will be enhanced in the process.

Though wise parents will set restrictions for their children's behavior, they will also give their children a great deal of freedom to move within the limits which have been prescribed. In his extensive study of self-esteem in children, Coopersmith found that the homes which produced children with high self-esteem were usually marked by a combination of firmness and freedom. Children should understand clearly what it is they may not do, but within the boundaries of what is permissible they should be given the freedom to live their own lives.

When major parental rules have been deliberately violated, parents should insist on firm but sensible enforcement of their rules. Wise parents, however, will tend to favor a positive approach in controlling their children, rewarding them when they succeed rather than punishing them when they fail. When some form of punishment is called for, sensible parents will not only use corporal methods like spanking but also, depending on the child involved, procedures like denying privileges.

How a child reacts to punishment is also important. If a child feels that a certain punitive measure is extremely unfair, the punishment will probably not correct his behavior but simply arouse resentment, thus doing more harm than good. Coopersmith found that children with high self-esteem are more likely to believe that the punishment they received was deserved than children with low-self-esteem (p. 194). The implications of this for a child's self-image are obvious. If a child believes that his parents are fair in their actions toward him and that they treat him with due consideration and respect, his self-esteem will be enhanced.

Christian parents will be particularly concerned to discipline their children wisely but firmly. Proverbs 22:6, though written many years ago, is still relevant today: "Train up a child in the way he should go, and when he is old he will not depart from it." Christian parents will also, however, be keenly aware of the difficulties involved in training their children. They will realize that they cannot fulfil this most demanding task in their own power. They will therefore pray for grace to heed the apostolic injunctions: "Fathers, do not exasperate your children, for fear they grow disheartened"; "You fathers . . . must not goad your children to resentment, but give them the instruction, and the correction, which belong to a Christian upbringing" (Col. 3:21 and Eph. 6:4, NEB).

Parents, further, should *encourage their children to become more and more independent* as they grow older. There are parents who prefer to keep their children submissive and dependent on them. This kind of treatment, however, hinders rather than helps the child in his quest for self-esteem. A good parent will try to let his children make more and more of their own choices. There are, of course, cases where parents cannot allow children to make their own decisions, or where they will have to overrule their children's decisions. But parents should make every effort to lead their children to make responsible decisions for themselves.

Children, therefore, should be permitted to express their personal convictions even on matters in which they disagree with their parents, to take part in family discussions whenever this is feasible, and to have their say in the making of family plans. In a home of this sort one may expect disagreements and arguments rather than perpetual sweetness and light—but the atmosphere which permits such differences of opinion will be more likely to produce children with high self-esteem than that of a home in which everyone is expected to agree with father or mother.

Haim Ginott makes a helpful distinction between giving children a choice and a voice:

Responsibility is fostered by allowing children a voice, and wherever indicated, a choice, in matters that affect them. A deliberate distinction is made here between a voice and a choice. There are matters that fall entirely within the child's realm of responsibility. In such matters he should have his choice. There are matters affecting the child's welfare that are exclusively within our realm of responsibility. In such matters he may have a voice, but not a choice. (*Between Parent and Child*, p. 60)

A final suggestion for parents is this: *Build up a child's self-esteem by indirect means.* A child's self-image is formed not just by what his parents say about him but by the way they say it. Percival Symonds, in his book *The Ego and the Self*, has some significant things to say about this matter:

Parents and teachers should be extremely sensitive to the attitudes they express toward children, just as children are sensitive to the attitudes expressed about them. It is important that children be referred to with warmth, appreciation, encouragement, and confidence, rather than with criticism, disparagement, and disappointment. Children respond not only to what is said to them and about them but also to the attitudes, gestures, and subtle shades of expression that indicate how parents and teachers feel. (p. 190)

To the same effect is the following statement by Sidney D. Craig:

During the child's formative years, his feelings of self-respect and self-confidence are determined primarily by the quality of his relationship with his parents. If the child comes to believe that his parents "see" him as a worthwhile person, he will perceive himself also as a person worthy of self-respect and of the respect of others. He will define himself as a person of value if his parents' words and actions toward him have helped to define him as a person of value. (*Raising Your Child, not by Force but by Love*, p. 101)

Ginott makes the point that our praise of a child should not have as its object the child's general character and personality but rather his specific accomplishments (pp. 33-36). When, for example, a child has done a good job of washing the family car, it is not particularly helpful to say to him, "You are an angel!" It is much better to say, "Thank you for washing the car. It looks like new again." The child's response will be to say to himself, "I did a good job. My work is appreciated." Praise of this sort enables a child to make inferences about himself which will enhance his self-esteem.

Christian parents should understand and accept what the Bible says about the way we who are in Christ ought to regard ourselves. It is of crucial importance that they see themselves as new creatures in Christ, who are walking by the Spirit's guidance and living in the Spirit's strength. Parents should then do their best to communicate these insights to their children, not just by what they say, but above all by what they are.

Chapter Twelve

The Joy of Christian Fellowship

Seeing ourselves in the light of the teachings of the Bible has important implications for the way we relate to others, particularly to fellow Christians. We have already explored, in chapters 8 and 9, the Scriptural injunction to accept and love our Christian brothers. How can this acceptance best be implemented?

Christian fellowship is one of the greatest blessings God permits His children to enjoy. It is hard for those of us who have never been deprived of Christian fellowship to appreciate fully what an inestimable blessing it is. Perhaps only a person who has been in solitary confinement for a time can really understand how much human companionship means. Dietrich Bonhoeffer, whose *Life Together* sets forth in an inspiring way what Christian fellowship means and how it should reveal itself, has this to say about the value and the joy of such fellowship:

> The physical presence of other Christians is a source of incomparable joy and strength to the believer.
>
> The believer therefore lauds the Creator, the Redeemer, God, Father, Son and Holy Spirit, for the bodily presence of

a brother. The prisoner, the sick person, the Christian in exile sees in the companionship of a fellow Christian a physical sign of the gracious presence of the triune God. Visitor and visited in loneliness recognize in each other the Christ who is present in the body; they receive and meet each other as one meets the Lord, in reverence, humility, and joy. They receive each other's benedictions as the benediction of the Lord Jesus Christ. But if there is so much blessing and joy even in a single encounter of brother with brother, how inexhaustible are the riches that open up for those who by God's will are privileged to live in the daily fellowship of life with other Christians!

. . . It is easily forgotten that the fellowship of Christian brethren is a gift of grace, a gift of the Kingdom of God. . . . Therefore, let him who until now has had the privilege of living a common Christian life with other Christians praise God's grace from the bottom of his heart. Let him thank God on his knees and declare: It is grace, nothing but grace, that we are allowed to live in community with Christian brethren. (pp. 19, 20)

Marion Leach Jacobsen, in her *Saints and Snobs,* puts the matter this way:

Wherever . . . the love of Christ has possessed a group of Christians its members will never forget what they experienced there—total acceptance, honest sharing, and genuine loving; a happiness that is overflowing, and a fellowship to which they can invite outsiders, knowing that when they come they will see the reality of Christ's love lived out in His children. (pp. 28-29)

What these authors have described is the way Christian fellowship ought to reveal itself wherever and whenever Christians gather. Unfortunately, the reality often falls far short of the ideal.

Keith Miller, in his well-known book *The Taste of New Wine,* has expressed the problem in the following words:

Our churches are filled with people who outwardly look contented and at peace but inwardly are crying out for someone to love them. . . . But the other people in the church *look* so happy and contented that one seldom has the courage to admit his own deep needs before such a self-sufficient group as the average church meeting appears to be. (p. 22)

And this is how Marion Jacobsen states the purpose of her book: "I make no apology for the premise of this book: many Christians do not find, in their local churches, the personal acceptance, love, and practical care God intended should be available there" (*Saints and Snobs,* p. 11). Mrs. Jacobsen goes on to say that although this is indeed a problem in the church, many church members either are not aware of it or fail to realize its seriousness:

Church-members like to think (and have others think) that loneliness, lovelessness, and snobbery do not exist among them. Those who vigorously defend the pure doctrines of the Bible and its way of life are reluctant to admit that in actual practice such social problems do exist among them. They would like everyone to keep his mask of spiritual pride and joy well in place instead of admitting that there is needless deep, humiliating hurt in the hearts of some of the church family. (p. 19)

Let us look at some examples of this lack of true Christian fellowship in the church today. Here is the way one woman described a visit to a church in a strange city:

I was a stranger in the city. The church sign read, "Welcome," so I went in. I smiled at the Sunday school children as they rushed to their classes. Neither they nor their parents greeted me. After I sat down, an elderly woman sat beside me. We exchanged names and shook hands. Another woman joined us, saying it was nice weather. After singing a few songs, we went to class. No one spoke to me.

After Sunday school everyone rushed to the worship service. The service included hearty singing, prayer, and a beautiful duet. The minister welcomed Mr. and Mrs. So-and-so. "I don't see anyone else I don't know," he said, and then went on with announcements. After the closing prayer, I waited expectantly to meet someone, but over a hundred worshipers filed out, not even pausing to say, "It was good that you came today."

Big words in the bulletin said, "Welcome, we are glad you came. Come often." But all I could think was, "I was a stranger and ye took me not in." (A. D. Schanz, "Was This Your Church?" *Power for Living*, Aug. 24, 1969, p. 3)

A black couple applied for membership in a white church. Though they were formally accepted as members, they never felt at home in the congregation. Aside from the pastor, very few people ever spoke to them, and they were never invited into a member's home. After a month or two, they stopped attending the church altogether. What was the use?

In a so-called "elite" church in the South, a group of girls attending the Sunday evening "fellowship meeting" deliberately made any girl of whom they did not approve feel so uncomfortable that she would never come back (A. B. Hollingshead, *Elmtown's Youth*, p. 246).

An American woman visitor, after having attended a service in an evangelical church in the Netherlands, tried to strike up a conversation with a woman who appeared to be a member of the congregation. The Dutch woman, however, drew herself up haughtily and said, "But I don't know you" (meaning, I haven't been introduced to you).

Fortunately, not every church is as unfriendly and un-accepting as those just described. But experiences of this sort occur often enough to give us pause. That these are not just isolated instances is shown by a recent report on membership losses submitted to the broadest assembly of an evangelical American church. The report revealed that among those who had left this denomination between 1964 and 1966 because they were dissatisfied with it, more than two-thirds complained about the clannishness they had found in the church. By clannishness they meant the unwillingness of its members fully to accept people from backgrounds other than those of the majority (*Acts of Synod,* Christian Reformed Church, 1971).

It may very well be, of course, that many of those who leave one church because they do not feel accepted will join another evangelical church where they do experience warm Christian fellowship. But it may also happen—and frequently does—that such people never come back to any church. They may have come to an evangelical church because they wanted to hear about Christ and His salvation. But because they were never really accepted by the members of the congregation, they stopped attending, and are never heard from again.

Surely we face a problem here which cannot be ignored. The situation is especially serious because if there is any place on earth where a person ought to find warm acceptance and loving fellowship, it is the church of Jesus Christ.

So the question arises, What can we do about this problem? What is the key to its solution?

Let us return once again to our main topic, the Christian self-image. As we have seen, to have a Christian self-image means to recognize ourselves as being in Christ—not just as individuals, but together with all other Christian believers. This implies the duty and privilege of recognizing fellow Christians as people who belong to us and to whom we belong in Christ. Only as we continue to live and act in harmony with that recognition will true Christian fellowship be experienced among us.

It would be difficult to find a better statement of this truth than the following words by Bonhoeffer:

> Christianity means community through Jesus Christ and in Jesus Christ. No Christian community is more or less than this. Whether it be a brief, single encounter or the daily fellowship of years, Christian community is only this. We belong to one another only through and in Jesus Christ. (*Life Together,* p. 21)
>
> One is a brother to another only through Jesus Christ. I am a brother to another person through what Jesus Christ did for me and to me; the other person has become a brother to me through what Jesus Christ did for him. . . . Not what a man is in himself as a Christian, his spirituality and piety, constitutes the basis of our community. What determines our brotherhood is what that man is by reason of Christ. Our community with one another consists solely in what Christ has done to both of us. (p. 25)

This, then, is the rock-bottom truth we must never forget: we belong to our fellow Christians through and in Jesus Christ. We do not need to ask whether we are related in any way to fellow believers. We are already related to them in an indissoluble way by virtue of the fact that we are in Christ together.

This leads us to another thought. If I am one with my fellow Christian today, I am one with him forever. Again Bonhoeffer:

> . . . If, before we could know and wish it, we have been chosen and accepted with the whole church in Jesus Christ, then we also belong to him in eternity *with* one another. . . .

He who looks upon his brother should know that he will
be eternally united with him in Jesus Christ. (p. 24)

Here is divine election in a new dimension. Election does
not merely mean that I am for all eternity one with Christ;
it also means that I am everlastingly one with my brother.
Just as it is impossible that the Christ to whom I belong
will ever let me go or give me up (John 10:28), so it is
equally impossible for me ever to give up the brother to
whom I belong in Christ. He may hurt me, sin against me,
cause me many heartaches—the fact remains that he belongs
to me and I belong to him forever! This indestructible "be-
longingness," which is an integral aspect of the Christian
self-image, must be the basis for our Christian fellowship.

We may get at this truth in another way. As Christians
we claim, on the basis of Scripture, to be one with Christ.
But it is impossible to be one with Christ without at the
same time being one with Christ's people.

Christ and His people are one as the head of a body is
one with its members. If, now, you hurt a member of a
body, you hurt the person whose body it is, whereas if
you do good to a part of someone's body, you do good to
the person whose body it is. So, for example, if you punch
my nose, you hurt me; but if you pat me on the back, you
are doing good, not just to my back, but to me.

Applied to the problem at hand, this means that when
we hurt a fellow Christian we are hurting Christ, of whose
body he is a member. On the other hand, when we do good
to a fellow Christian, we are doing good to Christ. How
vividly Christ Himself taught us this truth in the description
of the last judgment found in Matthew 25:31-46! To those

who failed to feed the hungry and give drink to the thirsty, the King says, "Truly, I say to you, as you did it not to one of the least of these, you did it not to me" (Matt. 25:45). But to those who did feed the hungry, give drink to the thirsty, clothe the naked, and visit the sick, the King says, "Truly, I say to you, as you did it to one of the least of these my brethren, you did it to me" (v. 40).

"See how they love one another!" is what people used to say about the early Christians. We envy the fellowship they had with each other—a fellowship so close that at times it even led to a community of goods. But what we sometimes forget is the reason for this close-knit fellowship: these early Christians knew themselves to be one in Christ in the midst of a hostile world. They were therefore truly one despite great differences—differences such as those between master and slave, rich and poor, prominent leaders of society and ordinary citizens, well educated and illiterate, Jews and Gentiles, old and young. It is only as we recapture this profound sense of oneness in Christ that we shall be able to experience the kind of fellowship these early Christians enjoyed.

We have been thinking about the basic insights which are essential to genuine Christian fellowship. We go on now to some specific suggestions which may be helpful to Christians as they try to put these insights into practice.

A word should be said in this connection about the question of our relation to non-Christians. As was stated in Chapter 8, every Christian is in duty bound to show love and acceptance toward every man, be he Christian or non-Christian. In this book, however, our primary concern is the view a Christian should have of himself and of other Christians. For this reason the suggestions which follow will deal primarily with the way Christian believers should accept and love fellow Christians.

My first suggestion is this: *We must have the right attitude toward fellow Christians.* Our attitude toward our fellow Christians must be determined not by what is or what we imagine to be their attitude toward us, but by our attitude toward God. Since God tells us to love one another, we must do so regardless of what we may think our brother's attitude is toward us.

Let us be very clear on this point. Our attitude toward others is a sure index of our attitude toward God. The Apostle John said, "If any one says, 'I love God,' and hates his brother, he is a liar; for he who does not love his brother whom he has seen, cannot love God whom he has not seen" (I John 4:20).

A loving, accepting attitude toward our fellow Christians can be maintained only through prayer. We must, therefore, be faithful in praying for one another, particularly for those in the Christian fellowship whom we might otherwise be inclined to ignore, dislike, or reject. Here again Bonhoeffer has a helpful word for us:

> A Christian fellowship lives and exists by the intercession of its members for one another, or it collapses. I can no longer condemn or hate a brother for whom I pray, no matter how much trouble he causes me. His face, that hitherto may have been strange and intolerable to me, is transformed in intercession into the countenance of a brother for whom Christ died, the face of a forgiven sinner. This is a happy discovery for the Christian who begins to pray for others. There is no dislike, no personal tension, no estrangement that cannot be overcome by intercession as far as our side of it is concerned. (p. 86)

Not only must we constantly be praying for one another;

we must also continue to thank God for each other. How empty life would be without the stimulation, encouragement, guidance, and joy that come to us through our Christian brothers! How we should praise God for the talents He has given other members of the Christian community— members who belong to us, and from whose gifts we may profit. Surely jealousy and envy between Christian brothers will not be able to survive when we continually give thanks for one another!

A second suggestion concerns *the importance of listening*. Commonly we think we can best help our fellow Christian by talking to him. Often, however, the best service we can render him is simply to listen to him. If, as the Bible says, we are to "rejoice with those who rejoice" and "weep with those who weep," we must be able to enter sympathetically into the joys and sorrows of our fellow believer. And we shall be able to do so only if we know how to listen to him.

It is important to know how to listen when we call on the sick. When I began my ministry as pastor of a city church, I used to worry about what I should say to the sick people whom I had to visit. Often I found myself preparing little talks for them as I drove to the hospital: "First I will say this, then that, then I will read such and such a passage from the Bible," and so on. I soon learned, however, that the most important thing a pastor needs to do when he calls on the sick is to listen. As I listened, I would sense what was the patient's biggest need at the moment, and then I would try to adapt my ministry to that need.

Sometimes there is nothing a lonely person needs more than just someone who will listen to him, who will lend a sympathetic ear. In such instances one might say hardly a word, and yet really help that person.

Attentive listening, however, is important not just for the sick and lonely; it is important for all our contacts with fellow Christians. The better we understand our Christian brother, the better we can love him and meet his needs. But we can come to understand him only by listening.

Note what a psychiatrist has to say about this matter:

> *Learn to listen deeply.* The art of paying attention involves stretching out your mind and heart and focusing on the other person with all the intensity and awareness that you can command.
>
> *Teach your ego to hold its breath.* All of us are self-centered much of the time. Each of us is an actor trying to impress an audience, to take the center of the stage. But if you want to pay close attention to another human being, you must train your own attention-hungry ego to stop striving for the spotlight and let it fall on the other person. (Donald E. Smith, "The Healing Touch of Attention," *Guideposts,* April, 1969)

Bonhoeffer sees attentive listening as an aspect of Christian discipleship:

> The first service that one owes to others in the fellowship consists in listening to them. Just as love to God begins with listening to His Word, so the beginning of love for the brethren is learning to listen to them. It is God's love for us that He not only gives us His Word but also lends us His ear. So it is His work that we do for our brother when we learn to listen to him. Christians, especially ministers, so often think they must always contribute something when they are in the company of others, that this is the one service they have to render. They forget that listening can be a greater service than speaking. (p. 97)

There is a kind of listening with half an ear that presumes already to know what the other person has to say. It is an impatient, inattentive listening, that despises the brother and is only waiting for a chance to speak and thus get rid of the other person. . . . Christians have forgotten that the ministry of listening has been committed to them by Him who is Himself the great listener and whose work they should share. We should listen with the ears of God that we may speak the Word of God. (pp. 98-99)

A third way in which we can implement our oneness with all fellow Christians is by *what we say*. We may begin by considering what things we ought not to say. How much harm is done to the Christian fellowship by words which are carelessly spoken—words which hurt, words which are unkind, words which are cruel. When we are tempted to sit in judgment upon our fellow Christian, we must set a seal upon our lips.

Bonhoeffer calls this "the ministry of holding one's tongue":

Often we combat our evil thoughts most effectively if we absolutely refuse to allow them to be expressed in words. . . . He who holds his tongue in check controls both mind and body (Jas. 3:2 ff.). Thus it must be a decisive rule of every Christian fellowship that each individual is prohibited from saying much that occurs to him. (pp. 91-92)

Where this discipline of the tongue is practiced right from the beginning, each individual will make a matchless discovery. He will be able to cease from constantly scrutinizing the other person, judging him, condemning him, putting him in his particular place where he can gain ascendancy over him and thus doing violence to him as a person. Now he can allow the brother to exist as a completely free person, as God made him to be. (pp. 92-93)

Someone has said that it would be well if everything we

were tempted to say about another person would not be said unless it could go through three gates. Over the first gate is written, IS IT TRUE? Over the second, IS IT KIND? And over the third, IS IT NECESSARY?

As we go on to consider what we should say to our fellow Christians, certainly we must always be ready to say the friendly word. A cheery greeting will often help to create an atmosphere of acceptance. When visitors or strangers appear in church, the least we can do is to make a special point of greeting them. Keith Miller, in his book *A Second Touch,* describes how much a word of love or concern might mean to people whom our lives touch daily, but whom we often fail to think of as persons. "I found," he says, "that just a question, an interested ear, and one might create a 'thirty-second island' of caring in a person's otherwise impersonal day" (p. 61).

Then there is the word of encouragement. Most of us need much more encouragement than we usually get. All of us, I am sure, do better work when people encourage us. Let us not be unwilling to praise people for specific ways in which they have helped us or contributed to our enjoyment. "Thank you for your solo"; "I enjoyed that offertory"; "Your class meant a great deal to my daughter"—comments of this sort may mean much to people whose efforts often go unnoticed. Young people especially need our encouragement, since they are rather easily discouraged.

We should be encouraging, too, in the way we talk *about* others. We may make or break a person's reputation by what we say about him behind his back. All of us know how a teacher's or preacher's usefulness may either be greatly hindered or significantly helped by what is said about him by others. Let us talk about others as we should like to have others talk about us.

A word of guidance may sometimes be needed. If it appears that a Christian brother is doing what he ought not to be doing, it may be necessary for us to warn him or to reprove him. Such reproof, needless to say, should be administered with the utmost delicacy, with respect for the brother, and in gentleness and love (see Gal. 6:1).

Once again we listen to Bonhoeffer:

> Reproof is unavoidable. God's Word demands it when a brother falls into open sin. The practice of discipline in the congregation begins in the smallest circles. Where defection from God's Word in doctrine or life imperils the family fellowship and with it the whole congregation, the word of admonition and rebuke must be ventured. Nothing can be more cruel than the tenderness that consigns another to his sin. Nothing can be more compassionate than the severe rebuke that calls a brother back from the path of sin. It is a ministry of mercy, an ultimate offer of genuine fellowship, when we allow nothing but God's Word to stand between us, judging and succoring. (p. 107)

But what is even more important in this connection is that we must continue to deal lovingly with a person whose attention has been called to some fault, or who may be in the process of being disciplined by the Christian community. Earlier it was noted that it is especially important for parents to assure a child of their affection for him at the time they are administering discipline. If children need this, so do adults. It is particularly at a time when they are being disciplined or reproved that our Christian brothers need our love and support. They need to be reassured that we shall not reject them but shall continue to pray for them and love them.

We must also be ready to bring a word of comfort. When our brothers and sisters in Christ are in any kind of trouble, they will need our words of comfort and consolation. Such words can best be spoken. But they can also be written. A short letter or note to a sick or bereaved friend will take but little time to write, but may mean a great deal to the person receiving it.

Finally, we are to show our love for fellow Christians by *what we do*. This includes, to begin with, a real effort to welcome newcomers. Mrs. Jacobsen, on pages 181-83 of *Saints and Snobs*, suggests a number of ways in which newcomers to a church may be welcomed. Here is one of them:

> When visitors who live in the area appear at a certain midwest church, two or three church couples in the visitors' approximate age bracket make a date with them for the next week. On the appointed evening they appear at the visitors' home bringing an entire meal with them—not only the food, but paper plates, napkins, silver, and whatever else is necessary.
>
> A meal is always the best kind of icebreaker, and the couples spend the evening together, giving the new people a taste of the warm fellowship that characterizes that church. (pp. 181-82)

We should always be ready to show hospitality, particularly to people who cannot "pay us back." This does not mean, of course, that we should not entertain relatives and friends, or that it is wrong to have a circle of close friends with whom we visit regularly. But we should be especially eager to entertain those who, though unable to repay our kindness, really need our hospitality. One thinks of such people as college students away from home, people who live in facilities that are inadequate for entertaining, single people, widows or widowers, married men whose wives are temporarily away from home.

As those who are eager to show our love to fellow Christians, we ought to be particularly concerned for people who might otherwise be neglected. Miss Corrie ten Boom, in her book *The Hiding Place,* tells a story which vividly illustrates the contrast between a non-Christian and a Christian view of people. While she was being interrogated by a Nazi lieutenant at the time of the German occupation of the Netherlands, she was asked to tell about some of her activities during the occupation, and began to describe her efforts to bring the gospel to some people who were mentally retarded.

> The lieutenant's eyebrows rose higher and higher. "What a waste of time and energy!" he exploded at last. "If you want converts, surely one normal person is worth all the half-wits in the world!"
>
> I stared into the man's intelligent blue-gray eyes: true National-Socialist philosophy, I thought. . . . And then to my astonishment I heard my own voice saying boldly, "May I tell you the truth, Lieutenant Rahms?"
>
> "This hearing, Miss ten Boom, is predicated on the assumption that you will do me that honor."
>
> "The truth, Sir," I said, swallowing, "is that God's viewpoint is sometimes different from ours—so different that we could not even guess at it unless He had given us a Book which tells us such things."
>
> I knew it was madness to talk this way to a Nazi officer. But he said nothing so I plunged ahead. "In the Bible I learn that God values us not for our strength or our brains but simply because He has made us. Who knows, in His eyes a half-wit may be worth more than a watchmaker. Or —a lieutenant."

Lieutenant Rahms stood up abruptly. "That will be all for today." (p. 166)

Visiting people in need is another way in which we can show our love. These include those who are old and alone, who are ill, who are recovering from surgery, who have had serious accidents. Included as well are those who have been bereaved, particularly after the busyness of the funeral is over and the lonely days have begun.

There are many ways of extending a helping hand to people. One way would be to bring a meal to a family which has just moved into a new house, or to a family where the mother has just come home from the hospital. Another way would be to help an older couple put up storm windows, or to help a younger couple paint their house. Still another way would be to provide transportation to and from church for a person who does not drive, or to bring someone to the doctor's office, or to take an older couple out for a ride in the country.

A final suggestion for promoting genuine Christian fellowship is this: let us do what we can to encourage the formation of small group meetings among church members. It must be admitted that both the size of many of our churches and the formal way in which we worship make it difficult for church members to get to know each other, to share their needs with each other, or to feel accepted by each other. Small groups meeting regularly in people's homes will do much to supply what is lacking in the regular church services. In meetings of this sort there should be a planned program of Bible study, in which all those present are encouraged to take part. But there should also be time for sharing needs and problems, recounting blessings, and praying for one another and for others who are in need. Such "household". meetings, when properly conducted, can help to deepen the love and care of Christian believers for each other, and to enrich their fellowship in Christ.

When the Christian faith is accepted in its totality, that faith brings with it a positive self-image. The Bible teaches us that if we are truly in Christ we are new men and women, redeemed from sin, accepted as God's children, and indwelt by the Holy Spirit. Though we continue to fall short of what we ought to be, we must see ourselves not as depraved and wretched beings, but as new creatures in Christ who are being transformed more and more into His image. Not only must we see ourselves in this way; we must do all in our power to help our fellow Christians have this view of themselves.

We are in Christ, however, not merely as individuals, but as members of His body. This means that when we belong to Christ we also belong to those who are in Him. We must therefore see our brothers and sisters in Christ as people to whom we belong, with whom we are forever one. Whatever we think, say, or do should reflect the fact that we are all in Christ together. Only in this way can we enjoy what must surely remain one of life's mountain-top experiences—the joy of Christian fellowship.

Bibliography

Bonhoeffer, Dietrich. *Life Together.* Trans. by John W. Dober-
stein. New York: Harper, 1954.

Branden, Nathaniel. *The Psychology of Self-Esteem.* Los An-
geles: Nash, 1969.

Busby, David. "Self-Image and Self-Esteem," in *Proceedings of
the Eighteenth Annual Convention, Christian Association for
Psychological Studies,* 1971, 6850 S. Division, Grand
Rapids, Mich., pp. 24-39.

Coopersmith, Stanley. *The Antecedents of Self-Esteem.* San
Francisco: Freeman, 1967.

Counts, William M. "The Nature of Man and the Christian's
Self-Esteem," *Journal of Psychology and Theology,* Vol. I,
No. 1 (Jan., 1973), pp. 38-44.

Craig, Sidney D. *Raising Your Child, Not by Force but by
Love.* Philadelphia: Westminster, 1973.

Cullmann, Oscar. *Christ and Time.* Trans. by F. V. Filson.
Philadelphia: Westminster, 1950.

Farnsworth, Kirk E. "Love Your Neighbor as Much as You
Love Yourself," in *Proceedings of the Eighteenth Annual
Convention, Christian Association for Psychological Studies,*
1971, pp. 60-62.

Fromm, Erich. *The Art of Loving.* New York: Harper, 1956.

Ginott, Haim G. *Between Parent and Child.* London: Staples,
1969; New York: Macmillan, 1965.

Glasser, William. *Reality Therapy.* New York: Harper, 1965.

——————. *Schools Without Failure.* New York: Harper, 1969.

Gordon, Thomas. *Parent Effectiveness Training.* New York: Wyden, 1970.

Hamachek, Don E. *Encounters with the Self.* New York: Holt, Rinehart, and Winston, 1971.

Hollingshead, A. B. *Elmtown's Youth.* New York: Wiley, 1949.

Jacobsen, Marion Leach. *Saints and Snobs.* Wheaton: Tyndale, 1972. Reissued in 1975 as *Crowded Pews and Lonely People.*

Lewis, C. S. *The Problem of Pain.* London: Collins (Fontana Books), 1957.

Maslow, Abraham H. *Toward a Psychology of Being.* 2nd ed. New York: Van Nostrand Reinhold, 1968.

Miller, Keith. *A Second Touch.* Waco, Texas: Word, 1967.

_____. *The Taste of New Wine.* Waco, Texas: Word, 1965.

Murray, John. *Principles of Conduct.* Grand Rapids: Eerdmans, 1957.

Ridderbos, Herman. *Paulus.* Kampen, the Netherlands: Kok, 1966. English translation by J. Richard de Witt: *Paul.* Grand Rapids: Eerdmans, 1975.

Rogers, Carl R. *Client-Centered Therapy.* Boston: Houghton Mifflin, 1951.

_____. *On Becoming a Person.* Boston: Houghton Mifflin, 1961.

Sartre, Jean-Paul. *No Exit and Three Other Plays.* New York: Random (Vintage Books), 1948.

Smedes, Lewis. *All Things Made New.* Grand Rapids: Eerdmans, 1970.

Stott, John R. W. *The Johannine Epistles,* in the *Tyndale Bible Commentaries.* Grand Rapids: Eerdmans, 1964.

Symonds, Percival M. *The Ego and the Self.* New York: Appleton-Century-Crofts, 1951.

Ten Boom, Corrie, and Sherrill, John and Elizabeth. *The Hiding Place.* Minneapolis: Viking Press and World Wide Pictures, 1971.

Torrence, E. Paul. *Gifted Children in the Classroom.* New York: Macmillan, 1965.

Index of Names and Subjects

Index of Scriptures